Rita Cahioro

Italian Americans

ETHNIC GROUPS IN COMPARATIVE
PERSPECTIVE • General Editor
PETER I. ROSE *Smith College*

Random House New York

Italian Americans

JOSEPH LOPREATO

The University of Texas at Austin

To My Parents *and the Other Lonely People
of Southern Italy* · COMPASSIONATE
MASTERS OF THE GODSPEED

◉ Foreword

"Nation of nations" or "Herrenvolk democracy"? Melting pot or seething caldron? How does one describe the ethnic character of the United States?

The conventional wisdom, reflected in traditional texts on American history and society, tells of the odyssey of one group of sojourners after another who came to these shores: some of their own free will and others in the chains of bondage; some to escape religious persecution, others fleeing from political oppression, and many seeking their fortunes. "Rich and poor," goes the story, "mighty and meek, white and black, Jew and Gentile, Protestant and Catholic, Irishman and Italian and Pole . . . a motley array who, together, make up the Great American Nation."

Although many a school child can recite the litany, even they know that it has a rather hollow ring. For most people there are at least three kinds of Americans: whatever one happens to be, the members of the dominant group (viewed differently depending where one stands in the status hierarchy), and everybody else. And, if one happens to see himself as a member of the dominant group, the number of alternatives may be reduced to two: they and we.

For a variety of reasons writers of textbooks and teachers of American history have tended to overlook or underplay this essential fact of American life. While acknowledging the pluralistic character of the social structure and celebrating the extent to which "our differences make us strong," they rarely convey the true meaning of membership in an ethnic group. And none know this better than those whose life experiences belie the notion of tolerance for all. Recently, a common plea has arisen from various quarters: "Give us equal time."

In response to such demands there have been attempts to alter the rather lop-sided image of American history and of the American people. Historians and social scientists have begun to respond to the call for a more accurate and meaningful view of race and ethnicity in America. Many have sought to "redress the balance," as they say, by upgrading the status of one group or another and rewriting their history to parallel that of the dominant group. One finds new volumes that appear to make the same strategic errors as those they wish to complement, i.e., placing emphasis on great events and prominent figures while avoiding in-depth descriptions of patterns of social organization, cultural traditions, and everyday activities.

Fortunately, there have been some other approaches tried recently, most notably studies seeking to reassess the entire ethnic experience not by playing the mirroring game (we have a hero, you have a hero; we have a holiday, you have a holiday; everybody has . . .) but by getting to the core of the social and economic and political realities of existence for the various peoples who came (or were brought) and stayed. The work of the latter scholars is far more important and, by its very nature, far more difficult. It involves new ways of looking, new perspectives. It encourages the examination of history and biography, of episode and event as before. But it also requires careful study of culture and community and character, the examination of everyday life.

Those who have and use such an imagination (C. Wright Mills called it "the sociological imagination") must possess a willingness to challenge the old homilies, to get away from stereotypes and deal with real people, and to relate that which is revealed with both detachment and compassion.

This volume is one of an original series written to provide student-readers with the sort of background material and sociological evaluation just mentioned. Like the others in this series, Ethnic Groups in Comparative Perspective, it offers information about the origins and experiences, the cultural patterns and social relationships of various groups of Americans. Taken together, the volumes in the series should provide a new and different look at the ethnic experience in the United States.

In planning the series it was decided that all books should

follow a relatively common format which would include chapters on social history, descriptions of social organization of the various communities and their differing cultural characteristics, relations with others and with the wider society, and a conclusion to tie the early chapters together.

The very best qualified historians and social scientists would be invited to join in the venture, those not only informed but committed to the approach sketched earlier. Each author would be given the freedom to work within the framework in his own way and in his own literary style so that each volume would be a unique contribution to the overall project —and each could stand alone.

Italian Americans is the first to appear. A glance at the table of contents will indicate how closely the author has followed the mandate. A perusal of but a single chapter will prove the book's uniqueness. Professor Lopreato, a native of southern Italy, is a scholar of both classical and contemporary sociology and the author of several related works, including the widely acclaimed study of southern Italians, *Peasants No More*. He is eminently qualified for this task and it was our good fortune that he was able to be persuaded to write a book especially for the series.

Italian Americans discusses the promise and the problems of immigration for Europeans in general and Italians in particular. It describes in detail the background of those who were to come (and those who stayed behind) and offers insight into the forces, both centrifugal and centripetal, that led thousands to leave *Il Mezzogiorno*, the South of Italy.

In succeeding chapters the author explains why the new arrivals eschewed farming and settled in urban areas where they, like other new arrivals, established close-knit ethnic colonies; how the Little Italies were, in time, transformed into Italian American communities; and how various indigenous institutions were modified by the American experience. He discusses Italian Americans as a group and as one of many groups that comprise the American nation and describes patterns of assimilation, achievement, and conflict.

Joseph Lopreato's volume is more than a story of immigration and adjustment. It is at once an analysis of an ethnic group whose members are correctly described as the archetypical new immigrants (most of whom came between the last decade of the nineteenth century and the third decade of this one) and a critique of the work of various historians and sociologists who have written on particular aspects of Italian American life.

Students and teachers will surely join me in saying *grazie* to the author for this new contribution to the sociology of American ethnic relations.

PETER I. ROSE
General Editor

◉ Preface

Two or three decades ago, when the Italian Americans were still relatively new on the American scene, an extensive literature developed about various aspects of the cultural transition of this very sizeable nationality group. But despite the fact that America's "digestion" of the Italians (as indeed of most of its other ethnic groups) is still in process, very little has been written about them in recent decades.

This book represents a sociologist's efforts to summarize and, where possible, bring up to date our knowledge of major aspects of the Italian Americans' social experiences as they bear on their continuing assimilation. Particular attention is paid to their social and economic conditions prior to migrating to these shores; to their reasons for migrating; their patterns of settlement; their problems of adjustment to the new society as they concern especially family relations and religious participation; difficulties of cultural contact with other nationality groups and with one another, when the regional divisions of Italy are considered. Finally, an effort is made to trace and assess their achievements in terms of education, occupation, and income.

I wish to express my sincere appreciation to Marilyn Bidnick, Ronald Birkelback, Nijole Benokraitis, and Sue Keir for their careful and accurate work as research assistants. Among other persons who helped in the preparation of the book, I am especially grateful to my wife, Carolyn Lopreato, and to Barbara Picket and Sherri Villemez, who gave generously of their time to typing and bibliographic chores.

My colleague, Walter Firey, took precious time to read the manuscript, make helpful suggestions, and give cordial encouragement. To another colleague, Leonard Broom, and his associates, Cora Ann Martin and Betty Maynard, go my sincerest thanks for their kind permission to borrow from their unpublished work on "status profiles of racial and ethnic populations."

Peter Rose, to whose initiative this book is due, gave painstaking attention to a rough draft of the manuscript. Whatever merit may be found in it owes much to his incisive criticisms and cogent suggestions on matters of content, style, and organization.

My greatest debt is to the late Professor Maurice R. Davie, friend and teacher, who first introduced me to the study of American minorities.

◉ Contents

Italian Americans

Chapter 1 ◉ Introduction

This book is a study of the Italians in America—their cultural characteristics before migrating to the United States; their reasons for coming; the institutions they developed upon arrival; their problems of adjustment to the new society; their aspirations; their achievements. Hopefully, the study of the Americanization of one ethnic group will lead to a little better understanding of America, its virtues, its shortcomings, and its promises. At the same time, an understanding of America as the *recipient* of immigrants will also cast light on the adjustments and transformations of those who have joined her, and this chapter will discuss the problem from this viewpoint.

The Promise of Immigration

Since 1820, nearly 45 million immigrants have reached these shores from all corners of the world. As a result, American society represents one of the most colorful and interesting human mosaics of all time. So heterogeneous is it that a student of ethnic relations recently described it as "a national society which contains within its political boundaries a series of *subsocieties* based on ethnic identity" (Gordon, 1964:37). The benefits accruing from such diversity may well constitute one of the greatest gifts bestowed upon a people by its history. They are clearly visible everywhere—in the most immediate aspects of the American's life as well as in the most remote. Consider the innumerable pleasures of the chef's art as one moves through the streets of our teeming cities or across the prairies and mountains that enfold the American Union. Or think of the richness and the challenge of our experiences as

we confront one another, across the veils and the grates of our
ethnic peculiarities, in the club, in the church, in the classroom, in the still circumspect adventures of a "mixed marriage." But if one would seek a more abstract benefit of diversity, consider the intricate beauty of American English as it is
twisted, transformed, and molded to capture the meanings of
experiences anchored in the roots of many cultural backgrounds.

A deeper examination of the importance of our great
differences reveals two even more dramatic advantages. In
the first place, as the Italian demographer Corrado Gini (1930)
once argued, there is some indication that closed, self-con-
tained, and inbred societies forever run the risk of biological
fatigue and deterioration. Through immigration, "new blood
enters the old organism," producing cross-breeding and re-
juvenation. In the second place, the great immigration laid the
foundations in American society for a sort of cultural rela-
tivism that is especially timely where complex divergences of
interests and ideologies are the rule. Poetic affirmation awaits
a people that can lay claims of kinship that reach in all directions across international divisions. The basis for cosmopolitan
wisdom and understanding is here.

Not that all problems confronting societies today are problems of misunderstanding. But more and more nations confront each other in anger not so much for what each declares
to be its interests and aspirations as for what *appears to be*
the interests and the aspirations of each. "Socialist" peoples
and "democratic" peoples keep each other on guard not because each wants to reach the "Great Society" or the "Just
Society," as the case may be, but because each believes that
the other intends to sacrifice one and all to achieve its particular approach to the Good Life. Increasingly, the destiny
of a people today is tied to the chance that others will not
impugn the honesty of its resolve or the essential benignity
of its aims. More and more, the compelling problem of peoples
is one of mutual trust and understanding.

The seed of international trust and understanding is deeply
planted in the United States of America where the citizenry,
professing varied national and cultural backgrounds, consti-

tutes in the aggregate a partial cross-section of the world's population. But whether the seed will germinate and thrive is a different question. One factor is of paramount importance. It concerns the skill that this society can muster in dealing understandingly and positively with its own human resources, its own complexity, its own internal differences. In endeavoring, therefore, a study of the experiences of one ethnic group in American society—the Italians—my hope is that the effort will be profitable not only in terms of itself but also in terms of what it may tell us about American accords and discords, our dilemmas, our strengths and frailties, our wisdom and stupidity, our egoism and altruism, and ultimately the success of our course within the family of man.

The Problems of Immigration

One thing is clear and should be recognized at the very outset: receiving and absorbing large groups of immigrants is not an easy social task. Although the coming together of different peoples and cultures can have regenerative and creative value, it is also capable of producing disruptive consequences, high degrees of social and personal disorganization, and a continual reorientation in the society's collective goals, moral traditions, and political structures.

The basic virtue of immigration is also its fundamental difficulty: it brings together, usually without prior preparation, very different peoples who are firmly set in their ways and who differ greatly in their aims and in their conceptions of the good and the bad life. It has been said time and again that man is a gregarious animal. His sociality, however, has a rather limited range. Man has not yet shown the capacity to extend his gregariousness to include all fellows of his species. To be sure, continuing expansion of man's social horizons appears to be a leading process of his history. While his social world once encompassed no more than a small circle of kin, and later a whole city at the most, for some time now he has extended his social vision to include the large aggregate we call the national state. In the process, however, he has developed new forms of association, new standards of evaluation, different forms of social relations. The nation is a group that unites under one banner but is not always united by one cultural experience. The significantly social phase of a man's existence still takes place within a small circle of kin and associates. And when he finds it necessary or convenient to "spread his wings" beyond his primary groups, the natural inclination is to settle among those who speak his own dialect, revere the same gods and traditions, observe the same etiquette, even exhibit the same skin color. In short, in the age of the United Nations, ecumenicism, and space travel, man's ethics and social habits remain largely tribal in nature.

ETHNOCENTRISM, PREJUDICE, AND GROUP CONFLICT. The factors underlying this tendency toward tribalism are numerous and interesting. One cluster of them is especially worthy of note. Writing within the tradition of evolutionary theory, William Graham Sumner (1906:16) pointed out that within the context of the "struggle for existence"—a process in which man and nature are the parties—men are also engaged in "the competition of life": "the rivalry, antagonism, and mutual displacement in which the individual is involved with other organisms by his efforts to carry on the struggle for existence for himself."

Ironically, this same competition of life is the focal point of association. It is the source of what Sumner most aptly termed "antagonistic cooperation," consisting of "the combination" of two or more persons or groups "to satisfy a great common interest while minor antagonisms of interest which exist between them are suppressed." The immediate cause of the cooperation lies in the fact that at a specific time and place the conditions and problems of life are the same for a number of human beings. The more fundamental cause is sociologically more profound. Says Sumner (1906:16):

> If one is trying to carry on the struggle for existence with nature, the fact that others are doing the same in the same environment is an essential condition for him. Then arises an alternative. He and the others may so interfere with each other that all shall fail, or they may

combine, and by cooperation raise their efforts against nature to a higher power.

The brilliant insight of the social-contract philosophers is thus effectively put to use by the sociologist Sumner. The resolution of open conflict limits the individual's freedom, but it also increases the chances of success for the group as a whole. At the same time, cooperation does not completely do away with conflict. The fundamentally divergent interests of the group members, or classes of them, remain. For one thing, some of them will get more benefits from cooperation than others. Hence, conflict is likely to flare up again and again. What is even more interesting is that through the renewal of open conflict—the "crisis," as Sumner calls it—men raise the society to greater complexity and to a greater level of power and adaptation to nature (Sumner, 1906:16). This is one of the most imaginative and productive discoveries of sociological theory: that conflict, whatever its costs, also has its positive functions. It stimulates the human mind to greater inventiveness and productivity. It has the power to stave off complacency, cultural atrophy, ossification.[1]

In the process of regenerative conflict, the group often increases its size—whether by conquest, natural growth through better living conditions, or immigration—and at the same time develops what a British sociologist once termed a "cake of custom." Implicated in a common set of life conditions, a group of people multiply and reinforce cultural bonds that hold them together. A differentiation arises, or becomes more marked, between that group and others. Plutarch noted some 2,000 years ago that different peoples honor different customs, but that all peoples honor the maintenance of their own ways. Each people begins to view things in terms that emphasize both the individual's loyalty to his group, the "in-group," and his contempt toward the "out-groups." Indeed, the antagonisms that are held at bay *within* the group are intensified, through a sort of compensating mechanism, and projected *against* other groups. According to Sumner (1906:13):

Each group nourishes its own pride and vanity, boasts itself superior, exalts its own divinities, and looks with

contempt on outsiders. Each group thinks its own folkways the only right ones, and if it observes that other
groups have other folkways, these excite its scorn.

For this view of things, Sumner used the colorful term,
"ethnocentrism," which is a major source of prejudice viewed
as "antipathy [toward others] based upon a faulty and inflex-
ible generalization" (Allport, 1954:10). Ethnocentrism is a
force that leads a people to exaggerate and glorify whatever
in their culture distinguishes them from other peoples. Their
folkways are the "right" ones. They have been sanctified by
tradition, religion, the heroic efforts of the ancestors, and of
course by the pragmatic demonstration of their worth. They
are culture, and that is sacred. Indeed, culture is often so
sacred that the great French sociologist, Emile Durkheim
(1915), was led to a near-equation of god and culture (or
"society").

What we have been discussing can best be observed in
fairly simple and homogeneous societies, the sort that travel-
lers and ethnographers used to find in large numbers until
several decades ago. The case of highly urban and industrialized societies is much more complex. Ethnocentrism here does
not involve merely one whole society in relation to another; it
may also involve relationships among sections or subgroups
of the society itself and their "subcultures." Culturally speaking, in a homogeneous society there are few "perceptual points
for alarm," and prejudices and antagonisms in such a society
are generally of two rather simple types. First, the people may
distrust and despise foreigners and strangers, whom they
may or may not know directly. Second, they may single out
for ostracism a few individuals because of imagined or real
peculiarities of behavior, just as the Hopi Indians ostracized
their witches or Two-Hearts (Simmons, 1942).

In modern industrial societies, conditions are abundant for
internal cultural struggle. Prejudice and conflict thrive on linguistic, religious, occupational, and other such differences and
inevitably occur when a new group of immigrants arrives
bringing in its own needs and aspirations, its own ideas of the
right and the moral. The intensity of the prejudice and conflict
that arise depends on several factors. The size of the incoming

group and the rate at which its members enter the host society are of critical importance. Robin Williams (1947:57–58) has enunciated the following theoretical proposition:

> Migration of a visibly different group into a given area increases the likelihood of conflict; the probability of conflict is the greater (a) the larger the ratio of the incoming minority to the resident population, and (b) the more rapid the influx.

Williams' proposition enhances an understanding of the Italian immigrants' experiences in America and should be kept in mind while reading the chapters that follow. Italians came in very large numbers. They also arrived at an extremely rapid pace. Little wonder that, as we shall see, they were for a time the focal point of considerable conflict in America and the objects of a great deal of ethnic prejudice. As we shall see, initially at least, the newcomers tended to react to these and associated circumstances by taking refuge in each other's company within densely populated ghettoes or "little Italies." There, they could cling more easily to old world habits and traditions as well as create, so to speak, an America after their own image. They borrowed what they could and retained a good part of what they would. Later, their children or grandchildren found a welcome in the outside world and in time moved culturally into the mainstream of American society just as they physically left the ghetto.

The break with the past, however, has not always been complete. In this, Italian Americans have followed a tradition of pluralism that appears to be deeply ingrained in American society. Half a century after the door was slammed shut and the massive waves of European immigration ended, American society still exhibits a great diversity of peoples and traditions that seems to defy those Americanizing forces once expected to produce the great American "melting pot." In nineteenth-century America there was a "belief that the United States was a melting pot in which Europeans were transformed into Americans by an almost mystical process" (Divine, 1957:1). In their study of five major ethnic groups in New York City, Glazer and Moynihan (1963:12) not that the powerful assimilating influences of the United States operate on all who live there: not only on the children of immigrants but also on the immigrants themselves, who will soon be "a very different people from those they left behind." However, the old belief that all traces of national origin would be amalgamated into a single new cultural type has as yet little or no foundation. Glazer and Moynihan find instead "some central tendency in the national ethos which structures people . . . into groups of different status and character" (Glazer and Moynihan, 1963:291). Ethnic lines are especially marked in this respect. The ethnic minorities of New York may even be considered *interest groups,* in the sense that various social and political institutions both "respond to ethnic interests" and "exist for the specific purpose of serving ethnic interests. This in turn tends to perpetuate them" (Glazer and Moynihan, 1963:310).

Reactions to Immigration

Why institutions of ethnic self-perpetuation came into being and are still sustained is a complex question that will be discussed in later chapters of this volume. One aspect of the question, however, deserves some attention at this point, although we shall treat it from a different perspective in the final chapter. There are three basic ways in which a group can react toward outsiders who seek to join it. One way is to change its ways to suit those of the newcomers. This type of response is extremely rare, if not altogether unknown, except when the new arrivals are conquerors who have the power to impose conformity to their ways.

A second reaction is to allow spontaneous and continuous syncretism whereby the different forms and traits of old-timers and newcomers coalesce in a union whose character owes a debt to all. By and large, syncretism is the invariable result when two or more diverse peoples and cultures come in contact with each other. But the process is rarely spontaneous.

Insofar as an effort is made, as it almost always is, to direct the process of "assimilation," a third type of reaction is likely to occur. The older group will seek to impose its own institutions and ideals on the new. So powerful is the human desire for acquiescence to one's own ways that the Italian sociologist Vilfredo Pareto (1935: section 1115 ff.) singled out a "need of uniformity" as one of the basic human forces impelling men to action. Naturally, the already established group in a receiving society is in a particularly powerful position from which to impose its view of things on the newly arrived.

It is likely that the need of uniformity has been especially strong in the United States. From the beginning, those who have peopled this country have been adventurers and seekers of the good life who have developed quickly a cult of gratitude to America and a deep sense of pride in its promises and opportunities. Throughout the centuries, many have been untiring champions of a promised land. According to those who came yesteryear to partake of, and add to, the blessings of America, he who arrived yesterday ought to give thanks to the good fates that steered him to these shores by hastily repudiating all previous allegiance and cultural endowment. Since no people is able to make a painless and rapid transition from one cultural world to another, the more the immigrant group was different from the old "American stock," the more it excited the wrath of the dominant group. This fact, in turn, tended to defeat the very aim of the receiving group: a quick annihilation of all that was peculiarly ethnic among the newcomers. For the period of adjustment required for a minority group's full acculturation and assimilation often lengthens in direct proportion to the degree of hostility displayed by the dominant group. The more violent the attacks against a group's traditions, the stronger will be its attempts to defend and strengthen those traditions.

Discussing the Americanization crusade that flourished in the second decade of this century, Milton Gordon (1964:106) argues that the "semi-hysterical attempt at pressure-cooking assimilation" was misguided because it ignored the stabilizing character of the immigrant's attachment to the cultural patterns and memories of the homeland and censured his alienness with thinly veiled contempt. The immigrants made certain necessary adjustments to the new way of life, but they resisted "the forced march tempo demanded by 'Americani-zation.'"

The "pressure-cooking" Americanization movement sprang up from fears provoked by the drastic change in the character of American immigration during the last decade of the nine-teenth century. The bulk of the immigrants began to come from southeastern Europe whereas most had previously come from the northwestern part of the continent. In terms none too generous to the more recent immigrants, the "old immigra-tion" yielded first place to the "new immigration."

The Italian Immigration

The Italians were the new immigrants *par excellence*. Of their total number, four-fifths came in the twentieth century. More-over, for every decade from the 1890s to 1930, Italy ranked either first among nations in the number of immigrants to this country, or very close to the top.

Italians have been in this hemisphere since the time of Columbus. But in 1820, at the first official enumeration of immigrants to the United States, only 30 Italians were re-ported. During the next sixty years, 81,337 more entered the country. Then in the decade of 1881–1890, the first substan-tial wave brought 307,309 of them to these shores. This figure more than doubled in the next ten years. The figures continued to mount. In the first decade of the twentieth century, 2,045,877 entered the country, and about half as many came between 1911 and 1920.

In the period from 1820 to 1967, German immigrants were first in number, with a total of 6,879,495; immigration from Germany was heaviest in the decade 1881–1890, when 1,452,970 Germans came in. Second in importance as a source of immigrants during the same period was Italy with a total of 5,096,204. Third was great Britain (England, Scot-land, Wales), with 4,735,489. Great Britain's highest total for a single decade was 807,189 in 1881–1890. Ireland had a total of 4,708,845 immigrants with immigration reaching a peak of 914,119 in 1851–1860. Austria-Hungary ranked fifth during the 1820–1967 period with 4,289,215 immigrants. Its largest contribution was 2,145,266 immigrants in 1901–1910 (U. S. Bureau of Census, 1941:109; 1968:92).

Only about 330,000 Italians have immigrated since 1930. The causes for the great deceleration of immigration are numerous. First, the Great Depression considerably changed the Italian's idea of the promised land. Not only were many potential immigrants discouraged by the constricted job market in America; some of those already here returned to the homeland.

The depression was hardly over when World War II brought Italian immigration to a virtual standstill. For a few years after hostilities ceased, considerable numbers of Italians came over to join those of their relatives who had conclusively cast their lot with America. Most of these immigrants had free access to this country by virtue of close family ties with others who had come before the war. In addition, 5,000 or 6,000 per year came by virtue of a special immigration quota allotted to Italy.

In the 1960s, opportunities for employment and achievement multiplied in Italy itself as industrialization proceeded in that country. As a result, many prospective migrants who before might have glanced westward across the Atlantic now find it easier to go to the booming urban-industrial areas of northern Italy, where reasonable wages in combination with relatively familiar cultural conditions attract people from the poor agricultural districts. Italian public opinion polls show that in recent years there has been a marked reduction in the Italians' propensity to emigrate (Luzzatto-Fegiz, 1956:1106).

Immigration Restrictions

The most important single factor in the reduction of Italian immigration to the United States was a set of restrictive laws passed by the United States Congress. To understand why these laws were passed we must first bear in mind that the first to emigrate in any considerable numbers to what is now the United States were the people of the northern and Protestant countries of Europe. It was they who patterned American institutions. These "old" Americans developed a mental framework that placed and ordered those who came later in terms of how closely they resembled the early settlers. As Glazer and Moynihan (1963:15) point out, the American mind had a place for the various immigrant groups, "high or low, depending on color, on religion, on how close the group was felt to be [to] the Anglo-Saxon center."

The coming of the Irish, beginning in large numbers about the middle of the nineteenth century, had aroused great antipathy and antagonism in the old Americans. For, among other things, the poor peasants of Ireland were predominantly Catholic. The newcomers from southern and eastern Europe were people often strikingly different from the "old stock" not only in religion but in language and appearance as well. Like the Irish before them, they also had very different political attitudes, educational standards, and personal standards of living.

The Anglo-Saxons were alarmed.[2] They knew that nearly 4 million Italians alone had entered the United States in the thirty-year period from 1891 to 1920. The fact that this huge wave of humanity consisted, in the opinion of many, of ignorant and illiterate peasants, paupers, criminals, and "riffraff" did not help matters. At a time when Darwinian doctrine had gained its highest acceptance in the United States, deep concern was also expressed about the allegedly great fecundity of immigrants from Italy and elsewhere in Southeastern Europe. Carl Wittke (1939:406) points out that even students of population statistics took no hesitation in "showing what disastrous results awaited a country in which 50 Roumanian or Italian peasants would have a perfect army of offspring in several generations, whereas the stock of 50 Harvard or Yale men would probably be extinct within the same length of time."

The fact that the Italians, like most others except the Anglo-Saxon immigrants, tended to come to the United States in throngs of males, rather than in whole family units, greatly added to the concern. A large proportion were "birds of passage," a relatively new phenomenon in the history of American immigration. Many came not to make America their permanent home but to earn a little fortune and then return home to invest it in a plot of land and other symbols of power and prestige that they had so much admired in their local gentry. If many Italians initially appeared to show little interest in the American ways and standards of success, it is not because they were too ignorant or indolent to strive for success, but because their drive in this direction, while implemented with American capital, was seen as beginning and ending in the home community. If they crowded the urban ghettoes and lived like troglodytes under the most wretched conditions, it was to a large extent because *they had not come to stay.* Their home was back in the old village. That was where, for them, time began. That was where life, however painful at times, had a meaning. There, too, through the jingle of the American dollar they would settle their score with the high and mighty who had inflicted on them all manner of abuse and humiliation and who might now be given medicine from their own cabinet.

Until the 1920s Italian immigration included one of the smallest proportions of women and children, and Italian immigrants displayed one of the highest rates of return to the homeland. During 1908–1916, 1,215,998 Italian immigrants left the United States to return to Italy (Wittke, 1939:437). The phenomenon of "the bird of passage" produced great anxiety and resentment among Americans of Anglo-Saxon stock. Here were throngs of foreigners who came and enriched themselves, but refused to bend their twig to the American wind. The restrictionist inclinations of the old Americans were reinforced, and Congress produced a series of severely restrictive immigration acts that to a considerable extent came to an end, for the time being at least, only in 1965.

IMMIGRATION POLICIES. The first general immigration statute (ending a previously laissez-faire attitude on federal regulation of immigration) was the Act of August 3, 1882 (22 Stat. 214). This act established a head tax on immigrants of 50 cents and excluded convicts, lunatics, idiots, and others likely to become public charges. Other restrictive actions followed, eventually culminating in the Immigration Act of February 5, 1917, which, among its other provisions, established an immigrant literacy test that had been recommended in 1911 by an Immigration Commission under the influence of great public pressure.

By 1921, the fear of an inundation of immigrants from the war-ravaged countries of Europe had given rise to a rash of Americanism that prompted Congress to act again. On May 19, 1921, the first Quota Act was instituted. This measure was intended to limit the number of immigrants from any given country to 3 percent of the number of American residents who in 1910 were found to have been born in that country. This "quota system" did not apply to certain categories of aliens. Spouses of United States citizens and their children under 18 years of age were exempt, for example. Few if any limitations were imposed on such "non-quota" persons. That is why the Italian immigration has been considerably larger than the allotted quota. The average number of Italian immigrants per year has been nearly three times the assigned quota.

The 1921 act established a total annual allowance for all countries of 357,803 permits, of which all but 3,000 were allocated to Europe. Within Europe, about 200,000 were alloted to northern and western countries. About 155,000 were given to the countries of southeastern Europe. As a result, in 1923–1924 total admissions (quota and non-quota) from southeastern Europe were 192,549; those from the northwestern parts of the continent were 393,342.

Italy, in comparison with what was to come, was still in a rather favorable position. Her quota was established at 42,057 (R.P.C.I.N., 1953:77), but the good fortune was of short duration. Soon, the year 1910 was no longer considered a good cut-off point between the old immigration and the new. The idea of "racial" purity was rampant. Robert Divine (1957:10–14) points out that in 1921 the argument had been that restriction was necessitated by the failure of the melting pot, causing a case of "alien indigestion." In 1924, the feeling was rather that "the melting pot concept was a fallacious

and dangerous belief which had created 'racial indigestion.' "
Accordingly, in order to further reduce the flow of immigrants
from southern and eastern Europe, on May 26, 1924, a new
Immigration Act substituted 1890 for 1910 as the base year,
and a 2 percent quota was instituted. This new legislation
reduced the total annual quota from 357,803 to 164,667.
Under the new distribution formula, 140,999 permits were
assigned to northwestern Europeans and only 20,423 to the
southeastern Europeans. Italy's quota was reduced to 3,845.

The 1924 act, however, contained a "national origins"
formula that was put into effect on July 1, 1929. Its fundamental assumption was that "the place of birth of prospective
immigrants is a reliable indication of their possible contribution to the United States and the likelihood of their becoming
good citizens. To those holding this theory the so-called old
immigrants from northern and western Europe are better
than the so-called new immigrants from southern and eastern
Europe" (R.P.C.I.N., 1953:91). The quotas were now com-
puted on the basis of the ethnic composition of the total
American population in 1920 as determined by a special exec-
utive board. The new formula provided a total annual quota
of 153,714, of which 150,491 went to Europe. Of the latter,
127,266 permits were allotted to northwestern Europe and
23,235 to southeastern Europe. Italy's portion was increased
to 5,802 (R.P.C.I.N., 1953:76–77), and it remained near
that level until the quota system was abolished in 1965.

Several more times after 1929, a legislative voice mocked
the famous legend on the Statue of Liberty:

> Give me your tired, your poor,
> Your huddled masses yearning to breathe free,
> The wretched refuse of your teeming shore.
> Send these, the homeless, the tempest-tost to me.
> I lift my lamp beside the golden door.

In 1952, however, President Harry Truman appointed the
Commission on Immigration and Naturalization and entrusted
it with the task of studying United States policy in this area
and recommending any action it deemed to be in the interest

of the country. The commission gathered prodigious amounts of information, holding public hearings in key places, and concluded "not only that the United States needs more manpower, but that the United States needs more immigration to fill this demand" (R.P.C.I.N., 1953:35).

What is more, for the first time a congressional body showed keen sensitivity to world opinion and to the needs of other nations. The commission found that United States immigration laws interfered with the implementation of foreign policy and with efforts to help needy nations. With respect to Italy, the commission specifically stated that "The failure of our immigration law to accord . . . cooperation [providing emigration opportunities] has, in the judgment of competent and objective observers, weakened the prodemocratic forces in Italy" (R.P.C.I.N., 1953:62). Addressing itself to the national origins system, the commission vigorously attacked three of its major assumptions: "(1) That there are inferior and superior races; (2) that immigration is harmful, particularly to the economic life of America; and (3) that the so-called 'new' immigrants have inferior personal qualities" (R.P.C.I.N., 1953:91).

Although the commission made enlightened and far-reaching suggestions for a new immigration policy, effective reexamination of U.S. immigration policy did not come until the early 1960s. On July 13, 1963, President John F. Kennedy strongly urged a new and positive immigration policy in a message to Congress. The series of actions and debates that ensued culminated, under President Lyndon Johnson's guidance, in the passage of a new Immigration Act on September 30, 1965. Among other things, this abolished the national-origins system as of July 1, 1968. Instead, the act limited annual immigrant visas to 170,000 (exclusive of parents, spouses, and children of United States citizens) on a first-come, first-served basis with a maximum of 20,000 visas annually for any one country (Kennedy, 1966: 137–149). The 1965 act represents a new chapter in the history of American immigration. It establishes new criteria of selection, based primarily upon technical skills in demand here and upon kinship.

A Note

Italian Americans belong to an aging ethnic group. In 1960 the median age of those born in Italy was 60.8, while it had been 56.5 in 1950, and 48.8 in 1940 (U.S.C.P., 1960:ix). Similarly, in 1960 the median age of the immigrants' children was 38.6, while for all native-born Americans it was 27.7 (U.S.C.P., 1960:31,6).

Still another clue that suggests that Italian Americans are aging is the fact that very little has been written about them in the last twenty-five years.[3] This circumstance has affected the nature of this book to the extent that it must necessarily emphasize early reports, and therefore the early conditions of the Italians in America. For more recent years, the nature of available census data inevitably focuses attention almost exclusively on the foreign-born and their children, for only these are singled out by the census enumeration. Finally, it has been impossible to find studies that distinguish between the first, second, and later generations.

Estimates of the size of the Italian American population vary widely. Monticelli (1967:20) suggests a figure of 10 million. Another source[4] estimated the total in 1963 at no less than 21.5 million. A third estimated that in 1950 there were some 7 million Americans, belonging to three different generations, who had at least one Italian grandparent (Livi-Bacci, 1961). There is in fact no accurate way of arriving at the exact number. However, considering the time of the immigrants' arrival, their average age at that time, and the rate of natural increase of the American population for each generation, it is almost certain that there are at least 15 million Americans who consider themselves to be Italian Americans.

Considering only those born in Italy (the first generation) and those of foreign or mixed[5] parentage (the second generation), census data indicate that in 1960 there were 1,256,999 in the first category and 3,286,940 in the second (U.S.C.P., 1960:31). In the same year 13.5 percent of all natives of foreign or mixed parents were Italian Americans, as compared with 13.7 percent for German-Americans, the largest group in that category (U.S.C.P., 1960:24–32). In 1960, 2.53 percent of the U. S. population was either born in Italy or born here of Italian-born or mixed parentage. If the third and later generations were included, the figure would probably be about 8 percent of the total.

Notes

[1] For a more detailed discussion of this question, see Coser (1956). Among other scholars who have deliberately stressed the positive aspects of conflict are Simmel (1955), Dahrendorf (1959), and, of course, Karl Marx.

[2] Robert Divine (1957:3) finds two other major factors underlying the move toward immigration restrictions that began in the last two decades of the nineteenth century. One was the climate of economic crisis that existed in the 1890s; the other was a widespread fear that the United States had exhausted its land supply.

[3] One could, of course, argue that this lack of information is partly due to the lack of Italian American scholars in the historical and social disciplines. However, several decades ago there were even fewer such scholars, and yet there was no scarcity of documents on the Italian Americans. Indeed, many significant studies were carried out by scholars belonging to other ethnic groups.

[4] An article in *Il Popolo Italiano* (a Philadelphia newspaper), reported in Monticelli (1967:20).

[5] Only one parent born in Italy.

Chapter 2 ◉ In the Home Society

What sort of people were the Italians who migrated to the United States? Why did they come? Where specifically did they come from? A brief examination of these questions will provide a basis for a better understanding of the experiences and the fortunes of the Italians in America.

Historical, Socioeconomic, and Geographical Notes

The convolutions of the history of the Italians provide insight into their recent behavior, including their emigration. What follows is necessarily only a brief sketch of a very complex story. To further simplify the task, the focus will be on southern Italy, from which the vast majority of our Italian immigrants came.

There is reason to believe that, under the aegis of Greek civilization, the southern Italians were generally prosperous and thriving. Beginning with the Roman onslaught, however, a succession of foreigners overran the area, causing continuous upheaval, widespread demoralization, and a series of violent transfers of property, among other things (Vöchting, 1955:32). The result was indescribable poverty. For the masses of people, ownership of land and all other forms of property became virtually impossible, and this condition remained essentially intact until the beginning of the nineteenth century, when feudalism, which in southern Italy exacerbated all other ills, was finally abrogated.

By the beginning of the sixteenth century, the economic and social difficulties of southern Italy had reached disastrous proportions. But they were to worsen still more under the ascendancy of the Spanish dynasty. A brief listing of some of the more critical wrongs perpetuated and aggravated by the Spanish Bourbons might include the following: (1) arbitrary laws that were never applied to the *gran signore* and other privileged individuals—indeed, in cases of quarrels between the mighty and the low, the former was all too often both the accuser and judge; (2) all manner of rights of pre-emption, banishment, and coercion that lent themselves easily to oppression of the governed masses by the ruling class; and (3) a system of excessive and abusive taxation.

The policies of the Spanish monarchs produced another disease from which the southern Italian people have still not fully recovered. Due to a never-ending obsession with the danger of conspiratorial activities, the monarchs always proceeded with the utmost severity against their enemies, whether proven or merely suspected. Conscious that the populace could not engage in effective political action without the nobles, and that the nobles needed the support of the people in order to act, the monarchs took every opportunity to create conflict between the two classes and to encourage disharmony among the nobles themselves. This procedure had the intended effect of weakening nobility and populace alike, impeding their agreement for any concerted action. It also augmented the ill will of the nobles vis-à-vis the populace. The end result of this policy of divide and conquer was generalized disintegration and demoralization. The masses were defenseless against the brutality and avarice of the nobles, and their hostility toward the oppressors was transferred into aggression against their own kind, causing ceaseless conflict.

The economic intelligence of the ruling class was not commensurate with its power. The principle followed was simple and incredible: cut down the tree before it yields. Toward the end of the sixteenth century, for instance, a new tax imposed on the exportation of silk was so heavy that it discouraged any further exportation of this product, and thus all revenues from it ceased. The production of silk was reduced to one-fifth of the original volume. In another instance, toward the end of the eighteenth century the duty imposed on raw silk from the region of Apulia was more than 50 percent higher than that imposed on imported silk (dal Pane, 1932: 50 ff.).

Under such circumstances, private initiative was quickly destroyed. When attempts were made to improve techniques of olive pressing, to plant potentially profitable trees, or to expand the cultivation of cotton, new and heavy taxes choked initiative at its birth, forestalling every attempt at innovation and improvement. To make things worse, rights of taxation and monopolies were often leased to third parties, who added their greed to that of the ruling class. The right of tax collection thus became a right of exploitation at two different levels of the privileged class (Arias, 1919:83).

Antonio Genovesi (cited in Vöchting, 1955:45) points out that by the beginning of the eighteenth century, 59 out of every 60 families did not own enough land in which to be buried. Hence, the peasant's ability to farm the land, such as it was, was almost entirely dependent upon the capital and the know-how of the landlord. But in the early 1700s a new evil arose. The landed aristocracy began a massive movement toward the cities, spurred by such factors as the recrudescence of malaria, increased government intervention in manorial matters concerning the rights and duties of the inhabitants of feudal lands, and the proliferation of economic and social opportunities in the cities. The impoverished peasants were left entirely without capital and farming guidance, and each pursued his vocation according to his ancient beliefs and with one goal overshadowing all others: minimize all risks in order to ensure survival.

The urbanization of feudal lords had still another deleterious consequence. When the nobles moved to the city, they entrusted the administration of their properties to overseers. Often these were ignorant persons motivated only by a desire to enrich themselves in the shortest possible time at the expense of the noble and the peasant both. Genovesi (1963) believes that the absenteeism of the feudal lords and the accompanying ascendance of the feudal administrator was one of the major causes of the agricultural backwardness of southern Italy, arguing that the peasants had neither the education, the spirit of enterprise, nor the capital to rationally cultivate the land. The peasants reached ever greater depths of disheartenment and inertia.

The invasion of the revolutionary French in the first decade of the nineteenth century brought a new era to southern Italy. In 1806, after driving the Bourbons into a brief exile, Napoleon installed his brother Joseph on the Neapolitan throne. During his two-year reign, Joseph attempted many administrative reforms, by far the most critical of which was the abolition of serfdom, made law on August 2, 1806. At that time, too, an agrarian reform was instituted, and some of the feudal lands were distributed to the landless. From the very beginning, however, the reform was ill-fated. Resistance to it by the landed classes was formidable. As a result, the peasants received very little land, and what they received was quickly lost again in many cases.

Writing in 1879, just as the migration flood was beginning, Giustino Fortunato (1911:88), one of the most illustrious thinkers on the *questione del Mezzogiorno* (the southern question), pointed out that those peasants who had been fortunate enough to profit from the distribution of state lands after 1806, had not yet surmounted their abject conditions; quite the opposite. The shares assigned to the peasants, which varied from 2 to 3.5 acres, were much too small to provide subsistence for a family. Productivity was low. The soil was easily exhausted. Taxes were high. As a result, one of three things generally happened: (1) the share was reclaimed by the town for unfulfilled payment; (2) it was sold for an insignificant amount to a large proprietor; or (3) it was surrendered to the usurer as payment for contracted debts. What remained was an immense reservoir of resentment and hatred (Fortunato, 1963:161), and indescribable "moral disorder" (Franchetti, 1950:171).

When, at the time of national unification, soldiers of the Italian army and Italian administrators entered such classical southern regions as Basilicata and Calabria, they found the population divided into three main classes of people: a small number of very powerful landlords; a group of lawyers too numerous for the needs of a land with very little industry and commerce; and a vast mass of landless peasants living in economic depression and semi-slavery. Very few were the peasants who owned a piece of land, and still fewer were the entrepreneurs, the artisans, and the intelligentsia capable of influencing socioeconomic conditions (Franchetti, 1950:55–56). After unification, moreover, the owners of extensive real property continued to adhere to the attitudes of the old landed nobility and disdained any form of commerce or manufacturing, while the other classes absorbed the mannerisms of their economic betters in this respect (Neufeld, 1961:147).

The political unification of Italy in the 1859–1870 period brought with it neither economic nor cultural unity. Indeed, the already underprivileged economy of the South was gravely damaged by national unification. Although prior to 1861 southern Italy as a whole had been a predominantly agricultural region, Naples and its immediate surroundings had become the seat of considerable industrial activity which, under reasonable customs protection, enjoyed relative prosperity. With unification, customs barriers were dropped, exposing southern firms to the overwhelming competition of northern industry. While the North profitted from accessibility to the larger national market (Saraceno, 1961:704), many of the previously prosperous southern firms had to be shut down, while others survived only at the cost of further exploitation of the worker (Vöchting, 1955:84).

As if all this were not enough, the new Italian state imposed additional and higher taxes on the population. The heavy debts contracted during the wars of unification now had to be paid. Further debts had to be incurred to finance the new administration, the organization of the schools, the expanding system of communications, and the army. United Italy, moreover, soon developed the tastes of a major power for engaging in foreign adventures. And such adventures, of course, were paid for by still more taxation. The impoverished South felt the brunt of the new taxes most bitterly.

PHYSICAL AND CLIMATIC FEATURES. Exploitation by the ruling classes and mismanagement of resources constitute one cause of poverty in southern Italy. The physical features of the region furnish another. One of the most striking facts about the South, a predominantly agricultural region, is the paucity of arable land. Although Italy as a whole has the rugged topography that is characteristic of all Mediterranean countries, the South is exceptionally rough. Italy has an area of about 75 million acres, of which 75 percent are mountains and hills. Less than 19 million acres of the total area consist of plains, and only about 5 million acres of plains are in the South. Stated otherwise, the farming population in the South represents about 44 percent of the entire farming population in Italy, but it has at its disposal only about 28 percent of the arable land. The remaining 25 million acres of southern Italy consist of barren hills and mountains whose geological composition grossly limits their agricultural value (ISTAT, 1963:2–3). It is ironic, moreover, that the southern mountains are high enough to be useless for agricultural purposes but do not possess sufficient altitude to provide the plains with a continuous supply of water from melting snows.

A look at a geological map of Italy reveals two outstanding features of the entire Apennines, from the Ligurian Sea to the Ionic Sea. The central band of these mountains consists of limestone, while flanking it on both sides are bands of clay and loam that go back to the tertiary period. The clays and the loams, in their extraordinary variety of forms, are especially prevalent in the South, where in some places they cover entire provinces (Fortunato, 1955:159–160). Such soil is characterized by a high level of impermeability, so that the plains of southern Italy are highly susceptible to erosion, with the topsoil being constantly washed away by the torrential seasonal rains that are another scourge of the Italian South.

The rugged topography of southern Italy and the impermeability of its soils would in themselves constitute tremendous obstacles for the poor peasant. But he has still greater problems. His difficulties are magnified by the aridity of his region. In some years, the summer is completely devoid of rainfall, and the drought may endure for six months or more. In the average year, the South has about fifty days of rain. But the rainy season coincides with the fall and winter, when the growth of most vegetation has slowed down or stopped altogether. Matters are made still worse by the fact that when the rains finally come, they often assume a torrential character from which only the ocean can profit.

THE ECONOMY. Nature thus has not been overly generous with the people of the Italian South, and their style of life has long reflected this circumstance. When they started emigrating toward the end of the nineteenth century, they left life conditions that were truly destitute. The typical peasant's home was a one- or two-room hovel, which he shared with his wife, three or four children, and sometimes a donkey, a goat, or a pig. But the whims of history and terrain, as well as the peasant's peculiar relationship to the land, involving excessive fractionalization, were such that his hut was then as now generally located, not on the land he worked, but in a village built some distance from the land, perhaps even high on a hill top. The peasant thus had to spend several hours a day walking to and from his several tiny strips of land loaded with his ancient hoe, a water receptacle, and a lunch that kept him lean but alive.

If by a supreme act of will and pride he succeeded in accomplishing a little work, too often it came to nought. After losing much of his produce to thieves, birds, diseases, landslides or drought, and paying an exorbitant share of the remainder to his landlord, the peasant usually managed to store only enough grain, fruit, or legumes to feed his family until early spring, months before the new harvest. At such time, then, he frequently could not avoid incurring debts that kept him in continuous bondage. There is every indication that in this respect things have improved in recent years. Yet, writing only a few years ago about Butera, a Sicilian community, Sciortino Gugino (1960:44) noted that usurers' interest rates are always higher than 20 percent and often reach 50 percent for a six-month loan, or even for a two-month period in the spring.

The peasant's situation, of course, was not always so desperate. There were times when a peasant cleared a reasonable profit from the sale of an animal he had assiduously cared for, and there were years when nature was generous, and he brought in a fair harvest. Assuming that he had no rapidly multiplying debts to pay, however, there was often a daughter to marry off, a lawyer to consult, an illness to be cured, or a funeral to pay for. Little wonder that as late as 1953 an Italian parliamentary commission on poverty (A.C.P.I.M.I., 1953) reported that 25.4 percent of the southern Italian farmers (excluding the totally destitute farm hands) could be classified as "wretched," while another 24.2 percent were classified as "needy."

The economic realities of life quite naturally had repercussions for the peasant's position in the status system of his society. His poverty was translated into social insignificance, subordination, contemptibility. As a sharecropper or farm hand, he was completely dependent on the capital of others for his very livelihood. Even as a petty owner, he had little wealth with which to exercise influence in a society that laid an enormous stress on social differences. Lacking the support and the leadership to organize a protest, the impoverished peasant traditionally sought to ensure his continued subsistence by practicing abject servility although this response was through the centuries the focus of general derision.

To make matters worse, the peasant had little or no schooling. At the turn of the century, 70 percent of all people in southern Italy above five years of age were illiterate (SVIMEZ, 1961:795). The percentage among the peasants alone was no doubt even higher. Poverty, illiteracy, and the resultant lack of power and civic participation made of the peasants a contemptible and ridiculous people. Writing as recently as 1934, the novelist Ignazio Silone (1934:30) dramatically portrayed their lowly status and their awareness of it. Speaking of the social hierarchy of a village in the Abruzzi, the peasant Michele describes the status of the likes of himself as follows:

At the head of everything is God, Lord of Heaven.
After Him comes Prince Torlonia, lord of the earth.
Then come Prince Torlonia's armed guards.
Then come Prince Torlonia's armed guards' dogs.
Then, nothing at all. Then nothing at all. Then nothing
at all. Then come the peasants. And that's all.

Writing only a few years ago, Anna Anfossi and associates (1959:171–172) argued that the century-old contrast between the *signori* (upper class) and the common people has given rise to a peculiar chain of invidious class comparisons. Each group tends to distinguish itself from the groups that it considers inferior and to imitate the attitudes and style of life of superior groups to the degree to which its finances permit, and very often even beyond. The social class that is most often used as a negative reference point is the peasantry. Thus the peasant is the mirror that all others use to admire their own superiority.

Until the turn of the century, the economy of the typical southern village was an extremely simple one, almost moneyless and nearly autonomous. Except for a handful of local gentry, which included usually the medical doctor, perhaps a pharmacist, the priest, the postmaster, the schoolmaster, and several municipal clerks, plus a dozen shopkeepers and artisans, the residents were all agricultural workers who tilled the land of the local *signori* or absentee landlords as tenants, sharecroppers, or farm hands. Perhaps a score or two were petty proprietors whose holdings had originated in the 1806 land reform.

Working 365 days a year, from sunrise to sunset, in a good year and when in good health, the peasants managed to produce the bare necessities of life after the landlord had been paid. Typically, the peasants produced a quantity of corn and sometimes a small amount of wheat with which they made their daily bread and their rustic macaroni; a few sackfuls of beans of various kinds, which substituted for meat in the diet (meat was a most rare luxury that could be afforded only once or twice a year); and various fruits, such as figs, apples, pears, cherries, walnuts, and plums, which were consumed in season or dried for consumption during the winter months.

In the small garden plot, the more fortunate peasants raised a variety of vegetables such as onions, potatoes, squash, tomatoes, and various greens. In less fortunate cases, the wife and children supplemented the supply of vegetables with gifts or earnings in kind, or with the many varieties of wild herbs growing in the fields. A handful of the more affluent peasants also grew a small quantity of grapes, which every year yielded a few gallons of wine, and a few quintals of olives, some of which were pickled for winter consumption and some of which were pressed to draw precious oil for cooking. All too often, however, olives and grapes were the exclusive property of the landlords.

Sometimes the peasant could afford a few luxury items. One of these might be a pig, which, if sickness and thieves permitted, would ultimately be sold in one of the nearby fairs and yield a little money for medicines or a few items of clothing toward a daughter's dowry. Or perhaps the peasant's wife and children would keep half a dozen hens that during the warm months would lay a few eggs to be sold at the market in a nearby town. Sometimes eggs might be consumed at home almost as a sacred rite during periods of illness. More frequently, however, eggs were given in homage to the landlord, or offered to the doctor in gratitude for his frequent services.

With the few pennies the peasant possessed, his wife made small purchases in the local shops: crude salt, matches, a little tobacco, some quinine to guard against malaria, an occasional liter of wine, salted sardines, on rare occasions a piece of lard or cheese, and still less frequently a few grams of sugar. Almost everything else that was needed, but not grown on the peasant's plot, was obtained through bartering his produce.

Farming techniques were archaic. The men tilled the land with a heavy, square-bladed hoe. Their women planted grains with a wooden dibble and weeded the field with a hoe similar in shape to that used by the men, but smaller and lighter. The plow, a single-share wooden implement, and perhaps the harrow were possessed only by a handful of independent peasants. Usually these peasants also owned a pair of oxen and an ox cart.

The peasants solved the problems of life by doing essentially what their ancestors had done before them. Life was viewed as an arduous affair that offered few comforts beyond those deriving from the inescapable knowledge that it could be worse. Except for an occasional chat with a neighbor or a periodical hour of religious participation, leisure was unknown to all but the very young, the very ill, and the very old.

THE CLASS STRUCTURE. Toward the end of the nineteenth century, the social structure of the typical southern village consisted of four major classes. At the top were the *signori* or *galantuomini* (gentry), comprising at most 1 or 2 percent of the population. They were the physicians, the lawyers, occasionally a titled aristocrat, the priest, sometimes a pharmacist or a teacher, and a few such others. The nobility, whether in residence or not, owned most of the land. Most of the remainder was in the possession of untitled *signori.*

A small number of craftsmen, shopkeepers, and minor officials made up what may be termed a middle class, which comprised less than 10 percent of the total. They lived and worked in town. This fact gave them a sense of superiority in relation to the peasants.

The bulk of the population consisted of agricultural workers. Around 15 percent owned a tiny plot of land, typically no more than five acres, which provided crops that were quite insufficient to meet daily needs; consequently additional land had to be leased from the landowners. Together with another 45 percent of workers who owned no land at all but leased it from the *signori,* these constituted the basic class, the agricultural proletariat.

The remaining 40 percent were the *giornalieri,* hired day laborers, the subproletariat, whose livelihood depended entirely on the whims of their masters and the seasons.[1] Even more than the bulk of the peasants, they led a life that some even today define as a "perpetual calvary." They were rarely employed on a steady basis. It was a life of *disperazione* and *miseria*—despair and misery; fear of man, god, and elements; dread of the future, hunger, and disease.

The policies of the rich and powerful classes, together with the most squalid poverty of the peasants and the cruel injustices inflicted on them, had, by the time of the great emigration, produced enormous problems. These were not strictly economic. They were more fundamentally problems of social disorder, rampant suspiciousness, and lack of trust in any but the most immediate kin. The kind of individual that developed through the centuries was a good candidate to enter the modern world of rational organization as a chronic misfit and alienated citizen.

For the wretched peasants, the chance to emigrate was a godsend. It was they who came to the United States. Of 1.9 million southern Italians who entered the United States between 1899 and 1910, 77 percent were agricultural workers, completely lacking the experience of work and life in an urban industrial setting. Less than .5 percent were in the professions, and another 15 percent were in skilled occupations (A.R.I.C., 1911:97). Such facts must be kept clearly in mind if we wish to understand the story of the Italians in America. For wherever the southern Italian went, he took along his historical, cultural, and psychological endowments. These included a long experience with poverty, which made the streets of New York look as if they were truly paved with gold; illiteracy; an expectation of great rewards from the new society combined with a deep suspicion of all legal and political institutions; an inability to cope effectively with an urban way of life; a great desire to strike it rich and then return home and become a completely independent farmer—and perhaps settle an old score with the rich and the mighty.

Causes of Emigration

To determine who the Italians were before they came to these shores is to gain an insight into the causes of their coming. In the last analysis, the Italians came to improve their economic position and thus eventually better their standing in their social world. But this represents only one set of causes, even if it is a fundamental one. Why the Italians felt compelled to leave their society in order to achieve this goal comprises another set of causes—indirect but no less fundamental.

The causes of any migration constitute a combination of *push* and *pull* factors. The first group consists of factors in the migrant's own society that, by undermining his opportunities for improvement, discourage him from staying there. The pull factors are those conditions in the receiving society that lure the migrant by sustaining his desire for self-improvement.

Considering the push factors first, the causes of the great post-1880 emigration include the pressure of population on the land; the miserable wages, amounting to only a few cents for twelve or more hours of work a day; infertility of the soil, combined with little or no risk capital and with primitive agricultural methods; poor health conditions in general and a terrible cholera epidemic in 1887 in particular; industrial backwardness or actual stagnation; a stubbornly lingering feudalism providing a jarring contradiction in a modern era; a system of heavy indirect taxation combined with an excessively high cost of living; an inexperienced, inept, incapacitated, and distant national government; corruption in local government; the secular exploitation by a privileged upper class. Perhaps more important than all these factors, however, was the cruel social and psychological punishment of the peasant by the master class and its satellites, to the point where to be a peasant, a *contadino*, in southern Italy was to be a stupid and despicable earthworm, an image accepted even by the peasant himself.

The pull factors are concisely summarized by Maurice Davie (1946:5–6), who argues that the reasons for immigration can be found in the differences between the countries involved. "The new country is attractive economically, politically . . . and socially; the old country is repellent in these respects."

Origins

The first Italian immigrants came from northern Italy. Most of these were farmers from rich Piedmont and Liguria. Upon reaching New York, a few who had sufficient means to undertake a long journey proceeded directly to the hinterland. They were especially attracted to California, where they developed rich citrus and wine enterprises. Most of the Italian immigrants conventionally attributed to the North, however, came either from the poorest agricultural regions of the Northeast (the Venetias) or from largely agricultural regions in central Italy like Latium or The Marches (Figure 1).

The fact that the first Italian immigrants to arrive were from the North is persistently but unduly emphasized in the literature. When the immigration from the South surpassed that from the North, there were only a few thousand northeners in this country. According to official Italian statistics, 772,792 Italians migrated to the United States between 1876 and 1900. Of these, only 99,023 were from the North (SVIMEZ, 1961:123).

FIGURE 1. *Regional Map of Italy*

No doubt the vast majority of those who arrived before 1876 came from the North, but these were so few in number that Italian sources make no effort at all to estimate emigration statistics for the United States prior to 1876. Nevertheless, judging from the yearly figures after the official enumeration began in 1876, it is quite apparent that the number must have been very small. Thus, between 1876 and 1880, only 13,235 Italians were directed to North America, and of these an undetermined number went to Canada (ISTAT, 1958:66). Furthermore, American census figures show that only 48,947 Italians arrived in the period from 1820 to 1874 (Bogue, 1959:351).

The vast majority of the immigrants have come from the poor agricultural regions of the South. Official Italian figures show that 5,058,776 Italians migrated to the United States in the 1876–1930 period. Of these, 4,034,204, or 80 percent of the total, were southerners, and only 1,024,572, or 20 percent, were from the central and northern regions. Looking at the regional distribution of the southern immigrants, we find, moreover, that 1,105,802 (27.4 percent) came from around the Naples area, Campania; 652,972 (16.2 percent) from Abruzzi and Molise; 300,152 (7.4 percent) from Apulia; 232,389 (5.8 percent) from Basilicata; 522,442 (13 percent) from Calabria; 1,205,788 (29.9 percent) from Sicily; and 14,669 (0.4 percent) from Sardinia (SVIMEZ, 1961:124).

Note

[1] For a more detailed treatment of the class structure, see Lopreato (1967:especially chap. 6). This volume is the source of much of the material used in this chapter. See also Moss and Cappannari (1962:287–300).

Chapter 3 ◉ Patterns of Settlement

Considering the facts presented in the preceding chapter, it is not surprising that extremely few Italian immigrants to America settled on the farms. At the present, about 70 percent of the entire U.S. population resides in urban areas, about 7.5 percent lives in rural farm areas, and the remaining 23 percent resides in rural nonfarm localities. By contrast, more than 93 percent of the foreign-born Italians in America make their abode in urban areas, and less than 1 percent live in rural farm areas (Velikonja, 1967:28).

Farming Eschewed

All sorts of explanations have been advanced to account for this pattern of settlement. The most common suggests that the finances of the immigrant when he first reached this country were a crucial factor. In 1910, the average Italian who arrived in New York had a total of $17 (Pisani, 1957:60). He could ill afford the expense of a trip into the hinterland, where the good farming land was, let alone the purchase of a farming plot.

It has also been pointed out that the Italian immigration was largely sponsored by the growing industrial and construction enterprises of America through their labor agents in Italy. These men tended to spread the word that only pick and shovel work was available across the Atlantic. The Italians, therefore, came to America allegedly predisposed to engage in manual work in an urban setting.

Constantine Panunzio (1921:77–78), a sociologist and an

immigrant himself, introduced the novel argument that Italian *contadini* were not farmers in the American sense; the work they did was more similar to excavation work especially in terms of the tools they used. He felt that this explained why so many Italians became construction workers in the United States.

There is an element of truth in most such explanations. All, however, leave much unanswered. Why, for instance, did the Italian immigrants, who had spent most of their life in the rural areas, not gravitate toward the farms and the fresh air once they had achieved a certain affluence in the city? Panunzio's argument is especially puzzling. It almost seems to affirm that the Italian *contadino* was born to dig, and nothing could divert him from it. Why then did he concentrate on urban digging and not on the rural style to which he had been accustomed, and which he could have certainly carried on in the new country?

There is one major weakness in the usual explanations of the Italian immigrants' failure to go into farming occupations. They all neglect the simple fact that *most of the Italians came to America precisely in order to leave agriculture for a while at least*. As Robert Foerster, the foremost American historian and keenest observer of the Italian emigration, argued in 1919, Italians did not travel to America motivated by a desire to obtain land and to pursue an agricultural occupation. However, the Italians did not reject farming, as Foerster hastily concluded, because they sought economic opportunities, which, when they arrived, were best in the commercial and industrial centers of the Northeast (Foerster, 1919:370–373).

While it would be senseless to argue that the Italian immigrant was less of an *homo oeconomicus* than an immigrant from any other country, Foerster's explanation of the Italian preference for urban life still lacks an important dimension. The evidence shown in the previous chapter should make it amply clear that the southern Italian *contadino* received few if any returns that could be properly judged rewards for his toils. Indeed, inasmuch as he was constantly on the brink of starvation, his work was punitive in nature. Since the peasant viewed himself as less important and admirable than the dogs of Prince Torlonia's armed guards, as Silone so vividly pointed out, farming was a punishment not only for his ill-nourished stomach but for his soul as well. It sickened his self. It humiliated his sense of being. It reduced him nearly to the status of the donkey and goat, animals that he constantly brutalized as an outlet for his anger. How could such a man be expected to go to America and court the risk of perpetuating the kind of life he had left behind? Should he go back home, so be it. He would return to that life, though he would then be economically better off and independent. But farming in America? That was absurd. The Italian peasant was much too clever to play a timid game with fate.

It is worth noting that even when the peasant was coaxed into undertaking farming ventures, he remained as stubborn as a mule. Both the American and the Italian national governments, as well as various American states and private agencies, actively supported the development of agricultural settlements for Italian immigrants in such states as Texas, Arkansas, Alabama, Mississippi, and Louisiana (Nelli, 1967: 43). All but a few of these ventures failed. And they did not fail to succeed because of the attendant hardships, as an Italian scholar proposed (Preziosi, 1909:81). Rather, it was because Italian peasants had had enough of farming. As they saw it, wealth, prestige, power, authority, luxury, all the symbols of a civilized existence, and even the sense of being truly human were associated with the style of life of their gentry. By taking up urban occupations, they performed a vicarious act of defiance against their former superiors. At the same time, they pursued the best road to achieving the economic means and learning the appropriate social skills with which to challenge the old *signori* upon returning to the old community.

There is an old notion deeply rooted in the fairy garden of scholastic romanticism that gets in the way of a proper understanding of the peasant's mentality and the motives underlying his self-uprooting. Ironically, this strange idea is best expressed by one of the most brilliant scholars on the subject of the American immigration. Discussing what might be termed alienation from factory work displayed by the European immigrant turned urbanite in America, Oscar Handlin (1951:78–79) waxes poetic:

> How could this man, so recently removed from an altogether different life, explain to himself the productive system in which he was enmeshed? Now he was a part of something altogether unnatural. It was that, rather than the length or laboriousness of his work, that was harshest. Indeed the factory was not at all like the field, the field over which he had once bent in piety, the field over which he had once cast forth the sacred seeds that would bring forth God's fruit on a morrow. At best, there was this cardinal fault in the new work, that it was separated from the soil . . . .

To careful observers of Italian immigration, this argument is sheer poppycock. Indeed, it seems amazing how much piety and religious reverence one can magically assign to peasants living in misery from the peepholes of an academic ivory tower. I recently asked an Italian American who had arrived in New York in 1907 what his first impression of America was, and he flashed back an answer that reveals clearly a deep distaste for the life of the peasant:

> I'll never forget the time my brother and I had just gotten off the ship, and we had an address to go to in Pittsburgh but didn't know how. There was a terrible confusion and nobody could help us. So, we slung our sacks over our shoulders and started walking. We didn't know a word of English. Then we saw a policeman standing in the middle of the street. Back in the old country we used to run anytime we saw the police. This one was smiling and came over to us. He said something, but all we could say was "Pittsburgh." Then my brother, who was nervous and scared, took a piece of cigar out of his pocket and started looking for a match. Believe it or not, that policeman took out a match and lit my brother's cigar. Can you imagine that happening in Italy? They would just as soon clobber you. Well, anyway, he walked us to the railroad station. On the way there, we stopped in front of a window and saw this huge chunk of beef on display. I had never eaten a piece of beef before . . . . I used to work from sun-

rise to sunset to eat wild herbs and beans . . . . I'll never forget how I longed for that chunk of beef . . . . My father used to say that peasants never die of starvation. But we almost did . . . . Well, anyway, New York was like a dream. We couldn't believe our eyes . . . . Pittsburgh wasn't so good, but there were plenty of exciting things to do. After work, those of us who weren't married would go downtown and live it up. Boy, what a change from that mud hole [the area he came from] I came from!

Little Italy

The Italian immigrants, then, settled in the cities, where they could most quickly make an economic gain and most effectively model themselves on those who in the old country had dominated their lives, exploited their labor, and degraded their mode of existence. But how exactly did they settle in the cities? Where? And under what conditions?

From the very beginning the Italians settled in what have suggestively been termed "little Italies." Italian immigration has always been a "chain" phenomenon. Whatever their reasons for migrating, the first to leave from a particular village became a nucleus of attraction abroad. Those who migrated after them from the same village tended to gravitate toward the places where the first to leave had settled. The reasons were many. Predominant was the need to be near someone who had to some extent solved the mystery of transculturation and could, therefore, help the newcomers adapt to the strange new life. Often those who had been first to migrate encouraged their fellow villagers to come with financial or moral assistance. Always the newer immigrants were attracted to a place by their need to see familiar faces and to hear familiar names and idioms.

It could even be argued that the Italian immigrant was culturally predisposed to settle in a "village" or a thickly settled neighborhood. Unlike peasants of many other countries, Italian peasants do not live on the farm where they work. They are urban farmers, so to speak. Like industrial workers, they traditionally have worked in one place and resided in another. Every day at dawn the country trails radiating out from the typical southern Italian village swell with a procession of workers bound for their plots on the sides of the distant hills. At dusk, the same trails come alive again in a never-ending ritual that is ultimately consummated in the village when the peasant consumes his much too modest supper. For the peasant, the village has always been the center of his universe. It is the microcosm in terms of which the macrocosm is ordered. It is the largest and completest whole. It is the only truly comprehensible whole. As Oscar Handlin (1951:8) notes, it is "the fixed point by which he knew his position in the world and his relationship with all humanity."

Even if the immigrant had preferred not to settle in the tenement and on the street populated by his countrymen and townsmen, he really would have had no choice, for when Americans discovered that the Italian immigrant bore little or no resemblance to Dante, Columbus, Galileo, Michelangelo, or Da Vinci, they developed a strong antipathy toward him that made the idea of having him as a neighbor utterly preposterous. Alas, the poor immigrant had nowhere else to go but to the slums that had already opened a door to his *paesano,* his townsman. Because the neighborhood was rat-infested and generally dilapidated, Little Italy also had the advantage of providing relatively cheap quarters that were an attraction to the destitute.

While the earliest immigrants had remained near their place of arrival for a time, eventually a few moved to different jobs in other towns and cities. Here their settlements formed new nuclei of attraction, and before long the newer immigrants had a certain margin of choice. Imitation Italian villages popped up in such cities as Detroit, Pittsburgh, San Francisco, and Chicago. However, most of the Italians settled along the eastern seaboard—in New York, and in the cities of Rhode Island, Connecticut, Massachusetts, and New Jersey.

The Italian "colonies" in all these places tended to be internally divided into "little Sicilies," "little Calabrias," and the like, and these in turn were broken down into "little Italian towns" from all over the Italian countryside. This tendency toward internal fragmentation reflected the fact that there had been little communication among the Italian provinces or even between one Italian village and another. Historical circumstances and the rough terrain had contributed to effective isolation of the various subdivisions. By the time the Italians came to this country, even their language was fragmented into innumerable regional, provincial, and even municipal dialects. Writing about "Little Hell," a "little Sicily" slum of some 15,000 in the Chicago of the late 1920s, Harvey Zorbaugh (1929:164) depicts this fragmentation:

> From the various towns of western Sicily they have come, settling down again with their kin and townspeople here, until the colony is a mosaic of Sicilian towns. Larrabee Street is a little Altavilla; the people along Cambridge have come from Alimena and Chiusa Sclafani; the people on Townsend from Bagheria; and the people on Milton from Sambuca-Zabut. The entire colony has been settled in like fashion.

However, while there was indeed a pronounced tendency toward segregated settlement, the pattern never developed to its logical extreme. The Italian colony was never even fully Italian. The Italians tended to move into neighborhoods that had previously been populated by such earlier immigrants as the Irish, the Swedes, or the Germans, who were now moving to other areas either because they had achieved greater status and affluence or because they wanted to avoid the problems associated with the recent arrivals. But not all of them left the old familiar tenements and streets. And other immigrants kept coming in. As a result, the little Italies were rarely if ever fully Italian, as was sometimes assumed. Nelli (1967:41) shows that between 1890 and 1920 the Italians represented more than 60 percent of the total population in only a few sections of certain Chicago streets. Indeed, their representation seldom reached as high as 50 percent.

The maintenance of the Little Italy depended to a very large extent on a continuous influx of new immigrants. For, as the old-timers achieved greater affluence and made a better adjustment to the larger society, many moved out of the overcrowded colony. Zorbaugh (cited in Nelli, 1967:42) noted in the late 1920s that, as the immigration laws of the time restricted the flow of new immigrants, the little Italies of Chicago were being dispersed and "fast becoming Americanized."

Living conditions in the immigrant colonies were hard. One of the oldest Italian settlements was "Mulberry Bend," New York's first Little Italy. A 1938 federal report (W.F.W.P.W.P.A., 1938:19) describes it as follows:

> Outwardly, a crooked three-acre lot built over with rotten structures, ordinary enough to anyone who simply looked at it from the street, the "Bend" lay within a maze of incredibly foul alleys. There the new arrivals lived in damp basements, leaky garrets, clammy cellars and outhouses and stables converted into dwellings. Every foot of the "Bend" reeked with abject misery, cruelty, shame, degradation and crime. By day a purgatory of unrelieved squalor, at night the "Bend" became an inferno tenanted by the very dregs of humanity.

Carl Wittke (1939:439) adds the following note on the little Italies of New York:

> In New York, Italians lived for a time at a density of 1,100 to the acre. . . . Twenty-five years ago, there were sections of New York City, in the Sicilian district, where 1,231 people lived in 120 rooms, and only Greeks and Syrians surpassed the Italians in the use of all rooms for sleeping purposes. The disease and death rate from tuberculosis was especially high. Local gangs terrorized the community. . . . Social life centered around the saloon, the cheap movie, and the dance hall, and the immigrant's most frequent contacts with Americans were through the saloonkeeper, the ward heeler, and the party boss seeking votes.

In his great classic of immigrant literature, *Christ in Concrete,* Pietro Di Donato (1937:137–138) paints a vivid picture of the sordid living quarters of Italian immigrants and their non-Italian neighbors. In the following passage, he describes a tenement house in terms that illustrate his inimitable talent for capturing concrete images.

> Tenement was a twelve-family house. There were two families on each floor with the flats running in box-car fashion from front to rear and with one toilet between them. Each flat had its distinctive powerful odor. There was the particular individual bouquet that aroused a repulsion followed by sympathetic human kinship; the great organ of Tenement fuguing forth its rhapsody with pounding identification to each sense. The Donovans' tunnel caught the mouth and nostrils with a broad gangrenous gray that overwhelmed the throat, but on acquaintance nourished into a mousey buffet. Missus Donovan, an honest Catholic woman, was old, cataplasmic, and sat for hours in the closet-small hallway toilet breathing in private heavy content, or at the front-room window munching her toothless gums. . . . The large Farabutti family in one of the upper flats had an oily pleasing aroma—the Maestro carrying with him a mixture of barbershop and strong di Nobili tobacco—and the children savoring of the big potato-fried-egg sandwiches which they chewed while shouting at cat-stick. The Hoopers had a colorless moldy emanation that hung and clung anemically but drily definite. The gaunt woman on the top floor who wore the gaudy old-fashioned dresses and brought men home with her talcumed herself stark flat white and left an insistent trail of old bathrooms littered with cheap perfumes. The top floor right—Lobans'— gave off a pasty fleshiness as though the bowels were excreting through the pores. Their breaths were revolting, and everyone in the family had snarling lips ready to let go profanities.

Functions of the Immigrant Colony

However gravely deprived the living conditions, these ghettoes had some positive functions. In some respects, they were even inevitable. Housing there was relatively inexpensive. Those who came in whole family units could rent, or share with friends, apartments at costs that, with some sacrifices, could at least be endured. Those who came as individuals could share a low-priced room with one or two others at a boarding house or at the house of a *paesano*. But more important still, life in a little Italy shielded the newcomer from the bewildering ways and demands of an alien and restless society. In an interesting biographical novel, Jerre Mangione (1942:164–165) points out:

> American morals bewildered my relatives. In Sicily their rules of conduct were well defined and though strict, fairly simple to follow, because the same rules had been used for many centuries and were known to everyone in the community, even to those who broke them. Here there were many different kinds of people and, as far as they could make out, no rules that were taken seriously. In fact, everything seemed to conspire toward the breakdown of the rules they had brought with them.

The functions of the immigrant colony vary according to whether we consider the goals of immigrants, the larger society's expectations of them, the duration of residence in the ghetto, or any of a host of other factors. If an immigrant group seeks assimilation into the larger society, then an extended residence in the immigrant community will hinder achieving that goal. Irvin Child (1943:44) argued that the tendency of Italians in New Haven to live in distinct, close-knit neighborhoods contributed to the preservation of "a distinctly Italian character." Whether a distinctly Italian character can actually be preserved is a point one may argue. Life in the ghetto, however, no doubt retarded mastery of those skills required for success in the economic, social, and political life of the city (Myers, 1950:367–372). It may be argued that, in general, when acculturation to the new society is the desired end, the immigrant colony is positively functional for the newly arrived but negatively functional for long-time residents. A lengthy residence within the ghetto indicates that the immigrant is failing to penetrate effectively the institutions of the new society.

During the initial stages of the immigrant's life in the new society, the immigrant colony performs very important functions for him. It works as a kind of shock absorber. At the risk of stating the obvious, it must be pointed out that, having uprooted himself from the old cultural milieu, the immigrant requires a certain period of apprenticeship in the social institutions of the new society. Having left his old society and being unable to make an immediate adjustment to the new, he finds himself on the margin of each but a member of neither. For a while at least he is a "cultural hybrid," a good example of the "marginal man." If the differences between the two cultures are great, the immigrant's problems are acute (Stonequist, 1937:3).

The two cultures that applied conflicting pressures to the Italian immigrant were indeed of greatly divergent natures. When he arrived, America was already at an advanced stage of industrialization. An industrialized society demanded forms of behavior totally foreign to one whose culture was deeply rooted in the soil, who was poorly accustomed to the idea of property and personal success, and who had practiced abject servility in order to secure his mere subsistence. The industrial social order was predicated on the ideas of individual success, of experimentation in moral as well as economic matters, and (what was almost incomprehensible to the Italian immigrant) of wanton competition. The immigrant was bewildered. Little Italy provided a means of bridging the gap between the old and the new. It was a sort of cultural incubator, a pot in which the old and the new were mixed together in a stew that prevented immediate indigestion and gradually took on an increasingly American flavor. As Stonequist (1937:85) noted, "The immigrant colony in America is a bridge of transition from the old world into the new; a half-way house on the road of assimilation."

Broadly speaking, the functions of a little Italy were twofold. On the one hand, because it was an imitation of the home society, it provided a comfortable anchorage point for the immigrant's continuing attachment to the old society and to its familiar ways of doing things. On the other hand, it was a place of ongoing transformation and Americanization. Ever in contact with the surrounding society and basically oriented toward it, the colony gradually absorbed elements of American culture. Little Italy then interpreted these elements to the new arrival in ways he could understand, and tempted him to accept them at a pace that was tolerable to his old world mentality.

In a recent note on the ghetto, Albert Kraus (1968:4), a journalist, has emphasized the economic advantages of this peculiar phenomenon. True: for those who were most meek, unfortunate, and bewildered, the ghetto became the last stopping place in a foreign land, "the ultimate backwater." But for many others, the ghetto provided remarkable advantages. Slum housing may have been dreadful, but it was also cheap. Getting to work by street car, subway, or foot may have been uncomfortable, but it, too, was inexpensive. Interest rates were most certainly high, but the money lenders, unlike the more respectable bankers, were willing to take risks in the ghettoes, thereby providing the funds that allowed an immigrant to set himself up in business. The earlier immigrants and their institutions usually helped the newer arrivals. It is a remarkable fact that the largest bank in the United States, the Bank of America, was organized and sustained by Italian immigrants in the slums of San Francisco's Little Italy.

Italian immigrants developed many institutions to help them in their new life and in their efforts to adapt their heritage to American conditions. As Robert Park and Herbert Miller (1921:119–126) pointed out in their classic on the assimilation of immigrants in general, certain business enterprises were developed by the most educated and venturesome to meet the practical needs of their countrymen. Among these were banks, travel agencies, employment agencies, boarding houses, import houses, real-estate firms, legal agencies, and the like. Also important were the mutual-aid societies. These grew out of the immigrant's desire "to die decently, ceremonially, and socially"; they offered sickness, death, and burial benefits. Out of these societies grew numerous lodges, orders, and fraternal and recreational organizations that gave the immigrant a valuable sense of security and a feeling of continuity with the past, and aided in the prevention of general demoralization.

From Little Italy to Italian-American Quarter

As previously noted, the existence of the immigrant colony as *a culturally unique entity* depends to a large extent on a continuous inflow of new immigrants. It is they who gravitate toward it, for they need it most. Italian immigration, however, has been only a trickle in recent decades, and the old-timers have either died or moved to more Americanized, less crowded, and more respectable neighborhoods. The little Italies, properly speaking, have all but disappeared. This is not to say that specific localities with great concentrations of Italian Americans no longer exist. As recently as the late 1950s, Herbert Gans (1962) studied the "urban villagers," native-born Americans of Italian parentage who, together with foreign-born Italians, constituted 42 percent of the population of the Boston West End.

In a purely demographic sense, many of old Italian neighborhoods have proved to be remarkably stable (Grebler, 1952: Chap. X). For example, New York City, with the greatest Italian concentration in the country, has a number of areas that have been heavily Italian since the early part of the century (Glazer and Moynihan, 1963:187–188). The Italian population of East Harlem, which has sent a number of Italian Americans to Congress and elected many others to city and state offices since the 1920s, shows a remarkable tenacity in the face of pressures from Puerto Ricans and Black Americans. Many sections of Queens and North Bronx have remained heavily Italian since the days when the immigrants fled the downtown ghettoes in search of cheap land on which they could build their homes and raise their favorite vegetables.

Willingness to live in a highly urban setting is no doubt dependent on one's conception of what constitutes a desirable residence. Italian Americans, like their relatives in the Old World, place a very high value on home ownership. One of the first acts of immigrants, when it seemed likely to them that they would remain in this country, was to purchase a house. Home ownership is the cornerstone of the Italians' conception of stability, respectability, and independence. This is no doubt tied to their unfortunate history. They rarely possessed land in Italy. Their labor was controlled and exploited by their masters. Their sense of dignity was often abused by any who had the power of the law, the gods, or the pen in his hands. But a roof over their heads—that was their secular privilege. The house was necessarily simple, but it was essential as an ultimate refuge. It gave the peasant what little privacy he had and allowed him to believe he was not absolutely at the mercy of others.

A large number of Italian Americans of the second and later generations feel as urgently as their parents the need to own a house, and, following the national pattern, some have moved to the suburbs. Here, indeed, their number is considerably larger than may appear, for many have Americanized their surnames and many women have married men of other ethnic backgrounds. In general, however, as Glazer and Moynihan point out, the Italian American's desire for the new and the fashionable in housing is restrained. Real estate in old neighborhoods adjacent to docks, factories, and railroad yards continues to receive, even if decreasingly, the approval of the younger as well as the older generations. Because of the pattern of urban expansion, they often find themselves boxed in, so to speak, between the business or industrial sections and newly developing areas. "Thus Italians occupy inlying areas that have been by-passed in the push to develop distant suburbs; in the shadows of the skyscrapers they enjoy quiet and convenient neighborhoods" (Glazer and Moynihan, 1963:188).

It is remarkable, however, how the old neighborhoods have been adapted to harmonize with the new economic affluence of their inhabitants. Tenements and single-unit houses may look dilapidated from the outside, but the interior shows great care and craftsmanship. There is almost always a great amount of skilled building and crafts labor in the Italian community (Glazer and Moynihan, 1963:187).

Italian Americans seem almost determined to perpetuate the thickly settled pattern of residence of the Italian countryside. Among the many factors that account for this situation, the desire for family interaction is especially important. The

Italian family, here as in Italy, exercises a very strong pull on its members. The most powerful magnet of all is the mother. For reasons that lie deep in Italian history, the mother has traditionally formed a powerful bond between herself and her children.

There is a certain parallel between the Italian mother-child relationship and the bond existing between the Black mother and her child. In both cases, the mother has had to protect her child from a harsh environment. In the case of the Black woman, one is reminded of Eliza in *Uncle Tom's Cabin* rushing her beloved child from Haley, the slave trader, to the dangerous hope that lay on the other side of the Ohio River. Moreover, the same system that tried to take her child away, only too often took her husband also. It is no surprise that if any family life was possible among the American slaves, it had to rest on the bond between the mother and her children. As a result, the mother-child relationship grew granite-like, and even today is by far the most solid relationship in the Black family.

Italians have never suffered slavery. Their environment, however, has been harsh. Until recent times, poverty, subordination, and insecurity tended to brutalize the peasant father of southern Italian society. His pent-up ire against nature and his lord was often displaced onto his wife and children. Four or five years after they were weaned, the children were often put to work and punished harshly unless they did their part competently and responsibly.

The mother became the child's chief source of comfort, his custodian angel, his staunch defender. In the process, she developed techniques of upbringing that instilled a strong and long-lasting sense of familial duty in the child. It is not uncommon to hear an Italian mother, wherever she may be, say to her child, whatever his age, that unless he does (or avoids doing) a certain thing, he will surely drive her to her grave. The Italian mother is so intensely attached to her children that she is usually quite in earnest when she declares "I'll die if my Johnny don't straighten up."

If one adds to her role as the child's protector the mother's boundless selflessness, devotion, and inexhaustible willingness to cater to her children's wishes and needs, it is easy to understand why the emotional bond is so strong between mother and child. Little wonder that among Italians there is no divinity, no saint who achieves the degree of popularity and devotion accorded the Virgin Mary.

The strong mother-child bond among Italian Americans is further strengthened by the mother's culinary art. On Sundays, on holidays, and on numerous special occasions during the year she is likely to prepare lavish dinners consisting of several kinds of meats, one or two types of *pasta*, special pastry, and various other delicacies that her children rarely learn to prepare or do not find easy to relinquish.

For all these reasons, the second generation has found it quite difficult to settle very far from the maternal home. But as members of the old generation die, and American ways begin to influence such matters as family roles and dietary habits, the intergenerational ties weaken and the dispersion of the Italian community increases. Already there are pronounced differences between the middle class and the working class in their attachment to the extended family. In a study of New Haven Italians (Lopreato, 1957), it was found that middle class Italian Americans visit other members of the extended kin group only slightly more frequently than their counterparts in the general population. By contrast, working class Italian Americans visit others in the extended family group almost twice as often as working class persons in general. What is even more revealing is that middle class Italian Americans are identical to the New Haven middle class in general in their expressed willingness to move away from the larger family. The Italian American working class, on the other hand, is about twice as reluctant as the American working class to leave the extended kin group behind. These findings seem to indicate that to a considerable extent the working class still adheres to old world habits and practices. The Italian American middle class, on the other hand, is for all practical purposes indistinguishable from the American middle class as a whole.

The second generation to a large extent and later generations almost *in toto* are, as we shall see, decidedly middle class people. This fact has clear implications for the cohesion of the Italian community. My prediction is that in the next decade or two, as members of the third and fourth generations reach independent status, Italian Americans will begin a massive exodus to the suburbs. Their move will be encouraged by the migratory pressure of Black Americans and other ethnic minorities on the Italian community.

In conclusion, maintenance of a little Italy, a highly fluid area essentially populated by the foreign born, was dependent on a continuous flow of new immigrants. The virtual cessation of this flow some decades ago gave the death sentence to Little Italy. In its place arose the Italian "section," "quarter," or "borough," whose existence depends largely on the solidarity of the bond between the old world mother and her new world children and on their reliance on certain special commodities (for example, certain bakery products) to which they grew accustomed as children.

In a broader sense, the existence of the Italian American community is dependent on its inhabitants' identification with at least some Italian American values. In an engaging book, Walter Firey (1947) demonstrated that where people live is not merely a question of economics, aesthetics, and the like. Spatial proximity among people has symbolic value. Space is an "instrumentality" in the sense that location within a given area is an expression of participation in the values that the members of a given group share (Firey, 1947:179).

Firey depicted the Italian North End of Boston as one such instrumentality. Contrary to some beliefs, the Italians who lived there had no apparent attachment to the neighborhood as a physical entity. Indeed, for some the area per se was plainly distasteful. It is a fact, nevertheless, that residence in it was instrumental to their adherence to certain cherished values in regard to occupation, family, choice of friends, group membership, availability of special foods, and so forth (Firey, 1947:179).

It follows that as values cease to be shared, the components of the ethnic community splinter off and dispersion occurs, even though it may take a long time before it is completed.

Dispersion is inevitable as immigrant-centered activities decrease and disappear. Significantly, Firey found that American-born Italians in the 1930–1940 decade accounted for a much greater share of the emigration from the North End than their parents. Looking at this question from a slightly different perspective, Firey found that persons in the 20–29 age bracket were much more inclined than older groups to leave the North End. To many of them, the district was undesirable as a residence because it had distasteful physical features and even more because it was associated with lowly status. As their children began to grow up, they looked to the suburbs as a more suitable environment in which to raise their families. In short, they were seeking identification with American cultural patterns (Firey, 1947:200–209).

Restrictive immigration policies, urban renewal projects, and the acculturation of the Italian immigrants and their descendants have taken a heavy toll on Italian communities. Italian Americans today are more aptly described as having distinct *regional* concentrations. Seventy percent of the first and second generations are concentrated in the megalopolis, the urbanized area that extends roughly from Boston to Norfolk (Gottmann, 1961).[1] The same area contains only about one-fifth of the entire American population. In 1960, New York City alone had 859,000 foreign-born Italians and their children. This figure represented 11 percent of the entire population of the city.

The extent to which Italian Americans are concentrated on the Atlantic seaboard is illustrated by Table 1, which compares the regional distribution of foreign-born Italians, native-born Americans of Italian or mixed parentage, and the entire American population for 1960.

It may also be noted from the table that the distribution of the second generation follows almost exactly that of the Italian-born, reinforcing the observation that the two generations tend to live near each other. A certain tendency on the part of the second generation to scatter more widely, however, is apparent in the case of the southern states, where the native born makes up a relatively larger percentage of the Italians

Table 1. Regional Distribution of Italian Americans and American Population as a Whole

Region	ITALIAN-BORN		NATIVE-BORN OF ITALIAN OR MIXED* PARENTAGE		TOTAL ITALIAN AMERICANS		ALL AMERICANS	
	N	%	N	%	N	%	N	%
Northeast	883,074	70.3	2,273,235	69.2	3,156,309	69.5	44,681,702	24.9
North Central	190,686	15.2	486,982	14.8	677,668	14.9	51,623,773	28.8
South	58,239	4.6	208,059	6.3	266,298	5.9	54,963,474	30.7
West	125,000	9.9	318,664	9.7	443,660	9.8	28,056,726	15.6
Total	1,256,999	100.0	3,286,940	100.0	4,543,935	100.0	179,325,675	100.0

* One parent born in Italy.

SOURCE: U. S. Census of Population: 1960, Subject Reports: Nativity and Parentage: Social and Economic Characteristics of the Foreign Stock by Country of Origin (Washington, D.C.: U. S. Department of Commerce, 1960), p. 8, Table 4, and p. 31, Table 9.

than in other areas. Among third and later generations, the regional dispersion is no doubt even greater but they, too, are probably heavily concentrated in the Northeast.

The Italians in America are decidedly an urban people; moreover, they overwhelming favor residence in the larger cities. A total of 88.2 percent reside in Standard Metropolitan Statistical Areas, and only 3.6 percent live in smaller cities. In 1960, each of twelve Standard Metropolitan Statistical Areas had more than 50,000 people of Italian stock (first and second generations only). Of these, the New York–New Jersey consolidated area had the lion's share with a total of 1,531,352. Next to it was Philadelphia with 248,558, followed in a gradually decreasing order by the Chicago consolidated area, Boston, Pittsburgh, Los Angeles–Long Beach, San Francisco–Oakland, Detroit, Buffalo, Providence, Cleveland, and Rochester. In terms of the proportion of Italians to the total population, in 1960 New Haven, Connecticut, was first with 15.8 percent, followed by Waterbury (14.3 percent), Stamford (11.7 percent), and New Britain (11.1 percent), all in Connecticut.

Note

1 And according to the 1960 census, 94 percent of all first and second generation Italians resided in the following 16 states: New York, New Jersey, Pennsylvania, California, Massachusetts, Illinois, Connecticut, Ohio, Michigan, Rhode Island, Florida, Maryland, Louisiana, Missouri, Wisconsin, Washington.

Chapter 4 ⦿ Social
Institutions and Change

This chapter focuses on the changes that have taken place in social institutions like the family and religion that have played a crucial role in the Italians' experience in this country.

Most Italian immigrants came to America with a cultural endowment that could not be preserved, except in its most superficial aspects. Furthermore, it did not prove very helpful for adaptation to the demands of the new life environment. Caroline Ware (1935:171–173) rightly noted that of the cultures brought to North America by various immigrant groups, none was in a weaker position to survive, much less to aid its bearers in the necessary transformation, than that of the Italians.

The linguistic problems of the Italians in America, perhaps more than anything else, bear witness to their culture's poor adaptability in the New World. The Italians were among the slowest to gain proficiency in the English language. The reason was not merely their very low educational level. Nor was it primarily their habit of living close to one another, where they were constantly tempted to keep using the old language. If they encountered severe linguistic difficulties in the new society, it was due in large measure to the fact that their language, however intrinsically complex, was geared to the expression of ideas that were ancient, almost changeless, and highly restricted.

For the southern Italian peasant at the end of the nineteenth century, the future rarely extended much further than the next sowing or threshing season. The past, in turn, always lived in the present. It was evident in the folk tales the peasants told, in the family memoirs the elders specialized in, in the black mourning garments they wore uninterruptedly, in the carefully preserved memories of cosmic disasters like droughts and earthquakes. Little wonder that even today the future tense among the southern Italian peasantry is virtually unknown and the preterit (what the Italian grammarians call "remote past") is virtually their only past tense. *Si levau 'u suli* (the sun arose), a Calabrian peasant will say even today to impress upon his family the fact that it is dawn. His time outlook may be expressed with the following paradigm: "X happened; it happens today; it happens always."

The things that happened, moreover, belonged to rather limited confines of experience. They pertained to birth and death, family and marriage, religion and the yearly crops, disasters and humiliations. The required linguistic tools were not very complex. Hence, the conceptual complexities inherent in the ethnically and religiously heterogeneous American society, which was gripped in the embrace of a future impatient to be and goaded by an economy in the process of radical transformation, were bewildering to the Italian immigrants.

As a result, for a long time, the Italians acquired only whatever little English was absolutely essential on the job. For the rest, they relied on the old dialects. These, of course, were not always appropriate. However much the immigrants were insulated from the larger society, they could not avoid involvement in a great many phenomena that had been outside their experience in the old society. New words and conceptualizations had to be developed. There had been no terms in the peasant's language for the English "shop," "store," "refrigerator," "factory," "car," "girlfriend." Even "street" had no precise equivalent, for what one had usually walked on in the old community was not really a street but a mud trail leading from the village to the farming plots on the mountain slopes. Thus a special American Italian language developed, heavily interspersed with "shoppa," "storu," "frigidaira," "fattoria," "carru," "gellafrienda," "streettu," and like terms.

The Family

Since the old culture proved largely irrelevant for life in the new society, the result of culture contact could only be a wholesale disintegration of the old patterns, and hence an initial period of disorientation. In 1930, Caroline Ware found the Italian community of Greenwich Village in New York City "almost wholly lacking in cultural coherence." She concluded that the breakdown of the old culture resulted from a variety of factors. But above all, she felt it could be "traced in the changing position of Italian women and girls." Various pressures operated in the United States to free women from the patriarchal bond, upsetting "their subordination to the group as a whole and to the man who was its dominant head." Then as now, many American institutions and organizations were designed to deal with individuals rather than with entire family units. The values underlying public educational institutions and recreational agencies and associations, the concepts of democracy and community participation, all rested on individualistic assumptions. Health agencies, recreation centers, church groups, all took the married woman out of the home and allegedly gave her a taste for autonomous action. Mothers were forced to "take responsibility for decisions about the children without deferring to the head of the house," and thereby were pried "loose from their positions within their family units." All this gave them "the idea of living for themselves rather than exclusively for the family group of which they were a part" (Ware, 1935:172–177).

Ware's emphasis on the changing role of the woman in the Italian American family may in part represent an echo of the powerful feminist movement of her time. The importance of the Italian patriarchal family is more fiction than fact. At the turn of the century, as now, women in Italy were quick to acknowledge their husbands as the family head but almost invariably had a strong hand in the important decisions of the family. Italian women have always been almost exclusively responsible for raising the children; attending to their children's religious education; preparing their children for marriage; articulating social relations with friends, kin, and townsmen; and above all, preventing the ever-present animus between father and children from erupting into open violence.

Ware was fully justified in emphasizing the radical transformation of the Italian family in the United States as a factor that accelerated the breakdown of the old culture. This transformation, however, is best understood in terms of parent-child relations. Ware herself (1935:174) tells of a woman who observed that the outstanding change in the life of the Italian community was "the loss of respect on the part of the children." This remark takes us close to a proper understanding of the changes undergone by the Italian immigrant's family and culture.

THE PEASANT FAMILY. One account of the Italian family in the United States, despite its brevity and certain apparent myths, can contribute a great deal to the present discussion. Paul Campisi (1948:443–449) has shown that the changes in the Italian family in America can be effectively viewed in terms of "a continuum which ranges from an unacculturated Old World type to a highly acculturated and urbanized American type of family." For the sake of convenience Campisi considers only three major types of all the possible variations. The first is the type of family that was transferred to America from southern Italy at the time of the mass immigration in the 1890–1910 period. This type is placed at the unacculturated end of the continuum. It is sometimes (cf. Ware, 1935:404) referred to as a "patriarchal" family. "Patriarchal," of course, is a term that can be quite helpful in grasping the essence of family organization in southern Italy, provided one does not use it to conjure up the extreme image of a group in which a man, usually the father and sometimes the grandfather, is the center of everything, omnipotent and omniscient. The typical patriarchal family of the southern Italian peasantry is rather a small group of unmarried siblings and their parents, closely knit together and disciplined to the idea that the major decisions of the individual's life ought to be made in accordance with the aims and the good of the group as a whole as defined by the oldest active member of the family.

In the language of Meadean sociology, the truly "significant others" of each member of the family are the other members of the family. While the group is closely linked to the other major institutional aspects of the community's life—religion, agriculture, education, marriage, sickness and health—the individual's role in each of them is mediated through, or entirely articulated by, the family group as a whole. In this sense, the family unit is to each individual member the basic "generalized other." One particular member—usually the father—is the figure that most readily conveys the essence of the whole. Ideally, he is a sort of quarterback on the family team. The shrewd observer will notice, however, that the plays he calls are often suggested or even diagrammed by another member of the team—very often the mother, not infrequently one of the older sons. In any case, the sense of mutual obligation is very strong. A member will think twice before committing an act that will weaken the powerful family.

The family group engages in a common economic enterprise, with certain provisions for division of labor according to both age and sex. All members of the family, including children scarcely ten years old, participate in the family enterprise, typically the cultivation of a small plot of land.

As long as the father is in good health and not too old, he is generally the task leader, apportioning jobs, decreeing what shall be done, setting up all necessary schedules. Whatever wealth is produced belongs to the group as a whole. The idea of work autonomy and separate gains is virtually inconceivable. It follows that involvement in an economy that is not based on family enterprise is likely to give family organization a radical jolt. The family unit has no provision for group solidarity on any basis other than common and collective enterprise. Little wonder that the requirements of American industry wreaked havoc on the Italian immigrant's family.

The family in southern Italy operated within the context of a society that changed very slowly. Hence the ties of the normal adult to the standards of the past were formidable. Parents saw it as an ethical duty to socialize their children in the proven ways of the past. The friends one made, the way one spent leisure time, the clothes one wore, the people one spoke to, the god and saints one revered, the kind of person one married, such things were in principle, and often in practice, all dictated by parental standards.

The question of marital choice merits special attention. It is not true, as it is sometimes maintained (cf. Ware, 1935:405;

Campisi, 1948), that the selection of a marriage partner was made by the individual's parents. Selection of a mate was indeed dictated by parental ethics and interests, but matters generally developed naturally in such a way that, when the time came, a choice satisfactory to all was usually made. Two sets of circumstances made this possible. In the first place, young ladies were strictly supervised and kept at a distance from all men except the very old and male members of the family, a practice intended to ensure that women reached the nuptial bed "chaste as the Virgin." Thus the young man could not manifest his amorous intentions directly to the woman, but had to approach her through the elders of her family. Moreover, the same moral principle that dictated strict supervision of the unmarried girl also demanded that the interested bachelor make his "intentions" known and "send for the girl's hand" through a member of his family or through a trusted family friend. This custom in effect demanded a union of two families as well as two individuals and had the function of ensuring a solid betrothal. The near-certainty of forthcoming marriage was required by the extreme emphasis put on female chastity, for although the engaged couple must avoid all physical contact, they managed somehow to show affection, and even this much lowered the chance of a proper marriage for the girl, should the engagement later be broken.

If the active involvement of the young man's family in his engagement was a sort of insurance for the girl's family that commitment to marriage was solemn, it also afforded his parents a chance to force consideration of the economic issue of marriage at the very outset of the courtship. In an agricultural economy as poor and precarious as that of the southern Italian peasant, there was intense concern to provide some economic security for a marrying couple. Depending on the area, there were certain things the boy's family gave him *in dote* (as a dowry) at marriage. But, given the extreme emphasis on virtue placed on a woman, her chance of "a good marriage" was always precarious. As a result, her dowry usually had to exceed by far the value of the groom's dowry. The involvement of the boy's parents in the engagement gave

ι chance to "talk business" early in the relationship.
ιcond set of circumstances making possible a choice
ιmarriage partner satisfactory usually to the entire family
unit concerned the fact that the choice was not a spur-of-the-
moment affair. Any family was likely to have special ties of
friendship, work interests, and the like with a number of other
families in the village. Marriage partners often were chosen
within this circle. Hence whole family units as well as the
marriageable youngsters had years in which to look each
other over. Generally, then, by the time the elders entered the
picture "to match" two individuals in marriage, the choice had
already made itself, so to speak. It is perhaps this sort of inevitability that underlies the old saying, *matrimoni e vescovati
dal cielo son destinati* (marriages and bishoprics are preor-
dained in heaven). Thus, although the young people usually
chose each other, parental authority and the principle that the
choice of a marriage partner was a family affair remained
intact.

Obviously, the patriarchal family organization could not be
maintained in the urban world, which was characterized by
a complex division of labor, intricate rules of behavior, and
unavoidably heterogeneous social contacts. Not only did the
family's inevitable and rapid breakdown symbolize the disintegration of the entire old world culture, but it was often
accompanied by extreme types of intergenerational cleavages
as well, as we will discuss in more detail later.

THE FIRST-GENERATION FAMILY. The second type of family
considered by Campisi is the "first-generation" family in transition. Some examples of this type still exist, but in general it
was a phenomenon of the first three or four decades of the
twentieth century. In such a family the foreign-born parents
were oriented toward the old ways, but the family also included their growing children—whether born in America or
in Italy—who had to adapt to the society of their future and
learn to cope with the differences between the standards of
the peasant family and those of the new society. The result
was often confusion, conflict, and disorganization.

Campisi lists numerous characteristics of the first-generation family, some of which are worth repeating here. By this time the family was only fictitiously patriarchal, and the father's previously high status was either no longer maintained or preserved only superficially. The family no longer constituted a tightly knit economic unit, and children were often an economic liability. Although children might be expected to work hard and contribute to the family income, they rarely met this expectation. The father no longer inspired awe and obedience. He was more likely to be loved than feared. The selection of a marriage mate was definitely made by the individual, although parental consent was still highly valued. Most of all, the solidarity of the family group was weakened, children were inclined toward individualism, and goals were no longer shared (Campisi, 1948).

In the early 1930s, Caroline Ware administered an interview schedule to 144 residents of Greenwich Village. Among other things, this interview gave them a chance to register their degree of adherence to the traditional Italian pattern with respect to marriage and the family. In a rough effort to assess differences between the old generation and the new, she divided her sample into those over 35 years of age, most of whom were probably foreign born, and those under 35 years, most of whom very likely were American born. Her findings, some of which follow, provide dramatic evidence of a deep rift between the two generations (Ware, 1935:193):

Does Not Believe That:	*Over 35 Years*	*Under 35 Years*
1. Marriages should be arranged by parents	70%	99%
2. Large families are a blessing	48%	86%
3. Girls should not associate with men unless engaged	45%	83%
4. Husband's authority should be supreme	34%	64%
5. A child should sacrifice his personal ambition to the welfare of the family group	31%	54%
6. Divorce is never permissible	12%	61%
7. Children owe absolute obedience to parents	2%	15%

The divergences between the two age groups are remarkable. The responses of the younger people represent a radical departure from the old culture in each case. To the extent that they concern very important, even sacred, aspects of culture, the differences reflect a deep cleavage between the old immigrants and their children. A point previously made is worthy of reiteration: the culture that the immigrants held out to their children was inappropriate for adaptation to the New World. It follows, as William Foote Whyte (1943:xx) found in his classic study of Italian American boys in a Boston district ("Cornerville"), that the younger generation has had to build its own society relatively independent of the influence of its elders. Indeed, the Italian born were the object of considerable ridicule on the part of the youngsters. The children were strongly attached to their parents; yet they looked down upon the "greasers." On the whole, the older people did not command the obedience from their children that the older generation received in most societies.

In the old society, the elders may have been considered severe, even hateful, but they were never deemed ridiculous. Why the change in the New World? To many of the younger generation, the old world peasants were obstacles to acculturation and success in the new society. As Oscar Handlin (1951: 243–244) so colorfully put it in reference to immigrants and their children in general, it was very difficult for the old-timers to show their children "the right ways around the twisting curves of the new way of life." The two generations belonged to two different worlds. "The initial dissimilarities of experience widened with time as youngsters ventured out from the home and subjected themselves to influences foreign to their elders. The life of school and the life of street completed the separation between the generations." The school especially was significant.

If it did nothing else to the child, the school introduced into his life a rival source of authority. The day the little boy hesitantly made his way into the classroom, the image of the teacher began to compete with that of the father. The one like the other laid down a rigid code of

behavior, demanded absolute obedience, and stood ready
to punish infractions with swift severity.

The school challenged paternal authority and undermined
devotion to Italian culture. While it no doubt aided the child
toward a certain accommodation with the culture that was
alien to his parents, it also encouraged him to reject everything
that was not American, and middle class American at that. In
so doing, the school also tended to build a false image of reality for the immigrant's child, as it always does for the lower
class child. Handlin (1951:246) vividly illustrates the fantasy
by reference to a widely used school book, *Good Morning, Mr.
Robin*. His discussion is worth noting at some length:

THIS IS JACK: THIS IS JACK'S HOUSE. THIS IS JACK'S
DADDY. JACK GOES SHOPPING: JACK GOES TO SCHOOL. ON
THE WAY HE MEETS A COW. ON THE WAY HE MEETS A
SHEEP. JACK COMES HOME. JACK FALLS ASLEEP.

And surely enough, across the top from page to page
the brightly colored pictures show it all. Blue-eyed and
blond, Jack himself stares out over the nice white collar
and the neatly buttoned jacket. Across the green lawn,
from the porch of the pretty yellow house, a miraculously
slim mother waves. By the side of a road that dips
through the fields of corn, the animals wait, each in turn
to extend its greeting. There it all is, real as life.

Except that it is all a lie. There is no Jack, no house,
no brightly smiling "Mummy." In the whole room there is
not a boy with such a name, with such an appearance.
One can walk streets without end and there will be never
a glimpse of the yellow clapboards, of the close-cropped
grass. Who sleeps like Jack alone in the prim room by
the window to be wakened by singing birds? *Good Morning, Mr. Robin*. The whole book is false because nothing
in it touches on the experience of its readers and no element in their experience creeps into its pages.

One could argue that the messages of such a cruel dream
were, for some at least, powerful stimuli for individual striving
and success—and to that extent probably beneficial. But one
wonders how many children learned to despise the foreignness

of their immigrant parents and to hold them responsible for their existence in squalid quarters far away from pretty yellow houses and green lawns. How many children learned to believe that daddy and mummy were grossly inferior to the man and woman who bought the pretty yellow house for blond little Jack? As the child grew older, he tended to reject his father—however lovable for his care and affection—as someone who could not furnish an example showing the way to personal maturity, self-respect, and social achievement.

The first-generation Italian family in America was thus characterized by intergenerational conflict. The conflict, of course, was not universal. There were exceedingly flexible, indulgent, and forward-looking fathers just as there were exceedingly pious, loyal, and understanding children. Moreover, as the children reached adulthood, parents, following an old country pattern, were increasingly inclined to look upon their children's standards as their own. In an early report on a Sicilian colony in Chicago, it was noted that, despite some misgivings, the old folks were letting the new generation "take the lead" and were "proud of their progressive sons and daughters" (Leavitt, 1921:158). Still, the gap between the two generations and their cultures all too often amounted to a veritable chasm. Two main differences between the generations almost invariably resulted in serious conflict. One concerned the language to be spoken at home.

Because they had little education and continued to associate primarily with others of their own kind, most old-timers never learned English comfortably enough to converse with their children in it. Therefore, they insisted that at home children speak Italian—or some variation of it. This demand was an obstacle to the child's attempt to learn English effectively. It also tended to give him a sense of separateness that he did not exactly cherish since he was usually oriented toward gaining acceptance in American society. In his enlightening reflections on his adolescent life in an Italian community of Rochester, Jerre Mangione (1942:228) discloses the immigrant's child's deep discomfort in this type of situation. He notes that "It wasn't that we [the younger generation] wanted to be Americans so much as we wanted to be like most people.

Most people, we realized as we grew older, were not Sicilians."
Moreover,

> My mother's insistence that we speak only Italian at
> home drew a sharp line between our existence there and
> our life in the world outside. We gradually acquired the
> notion that we were Italian at home and American (what-
> ever that was) elsewhere. Instinctively, we all sensed the
> necessity of adapting ourselves to two different worlds
> (Mangione, 1942:52).

That was more easily said than done. The two different worlds
could have been brought together comfortably within one
consciousness if they had shown willing points of contact.
All too often, however, the two worlds pulled in different
directions, with the result that the cultural muscle of the
second generation was greatly strained.

The second, more fundamental, difference between the two
generations concerned marriage. Handlin (1951:255) argued
that the "ultimate barrier" between immigrants and their children in general was that "they would never understand each
other's conception of marriage." In the case of the Italians
the parents basically viewed marriage as a means of extending
in time the continuity of the family. It was, therefore, a family
affair, and the child ought to adapt his personal inclinations to
those of the family group as a whole. Because it was a family
concern, a tie of marriage was best contracted between two
individuals whose respective family groups were in harmony
to some extent. A member of a family from the old village,
or at least from somewhere in Italy, was the natural preference of the parents. Marriage with strangers and members of
other nationalities was to be avoided. The customs and morals
of these other people baffled, bewildered, and frightened the
old folks. The immigrants' children, however, were influenced
by the ideals of the American institution of marriage, with all
its emphasis on individual choice, romance, love. Moreover,
given their tendency to disapprove of the old world culture,
marriage was often viewed by the younger people as an
act of liberation from the old family ties.

Intergenerational discord was great. It was particularly

harsh when the immigrant's daughter was involved. In the Old World, a girl beyond childhood was closely supervised by the family, and her contacts with available bachelors were at a minimum or altogether nonexistent. When the time for marriage came, a spouse was found through the direct or indirect intervention of someone in the kin group. In the New World it was not easy to supervise the girls, who often worked some distance from home with no kin present. Nor was it usually possible for the family group to help find them a spouse. Yet many of the old folks continued to restrict the daughters' independent efforts to find a husband even when they no longer had the power to help find one for them (Ware, 1935:182).

Such a situation naturally bred resentment and conflict within the family group. Nevertheless, saying that the generations were in conflict is not equivalent to saying that the children of immigrants invariably went their own way. The Italian family was much too solid and it was much too sacred to the average individual to tolerate unabridgeable emotional differences between its members. The heavy concentration of Italian Americans of several generations in a few states suggests a high degree of continuing family solidarity in this ethnic group.

When the generations clash on cultural grounds—whether because of the natural process of cultural change within a society or because of the conflicting pressures generated by migration—various forms of adaptation are open to the second generation. Irvin Child's (1943) study of "the second generation in conflict" in New Haven, Connecticut, is enlightening in this respect. Child sought to isolate different types of individual adjustment to American culture among Italian immigrants' sons, who had been either born in America or brought from the old country at an early age. Child's study is relevant here because, though he focused on second-generation individuals, apparently most of them were still members of first-generation families.

Child began by pointing out that the second-generation individual was socialized under the impact of two different and largely incompatible cultures, thereby acquiring conflicting goals, habits, and attitudes. Hence, the individual could be viewed as being in a state of "double approach–avoidance conflict" in which he was faced with two possible courses of action, "from each of which both rewards and punishments are anticipated" depending on whether conformity was to one or the other culture (Child, 1943:67). Child saw three major types of reaction to this conflict-laden situation: the "rebel," the "in-group," and the "apathetic" reactions.

Individuals who display the *rebel* reaction tend to eschew membership in the Italian group and to seek instead complete acceptance by the American group. "Attainment of this goal requires that the individual rid himself of habits and associations that mark him as Italian and become as completely as possible an American" (Child, 1943:76). The rebel is the individual who, asked whether he thinks of himself as an Italian, an American, or an Italian American, answers that he is an American, has "no leanings and likes for the old country," and regards "the Italians of the old country as a separate race."

Given his intense desire to be considered an American rather than a member of an Italian group, the rebel is particularly likely to be hurt when he is referred to by any of the ethnic epithets common in his area. He condemns Italians who are organized into "ethnic clubs" and reports a relatively large proportion of non-Italian friends. In searching for a wife, he either favors a girl outside his nationality group or a girl of Italian extraction who is well educated, "broadminded," and well disposed toward "the American way of life." Not infrequently, he marries early in order to break away from the parental family. More often still, he is in bitter conflict with the parental family, blaming the old folks for his inability to feel completely American or to achieve a fully American status. He is likely to consider it ill advised, ill bred, and ill educated to speak Italian outside the home unless perhaps it be "real" Italian rather than the provincial dialect his old folks are likely to know.

The rebel is frustrated by the larger society's prejudice toward him, but despite all barriers he continues his effort to become a "real" American. Indeed, the most outstanding characteristic of the rebel is his impatience to become thoroughly American *in the shortest period possible.* Coupled with it is anger at the Italians for their failure to be more quickly Americanized, and at the Americans for their disinterest in distinguishing between dfferent types of Italian Americans (Child, 1943:chap. 4).

Child does not indicate the proportion of second-generation Italians who exhibited the rebel reaction. I would guess, however, that in the United States as a whole this type of adaptation has always represented a minority, perhaps no more than one-fourth of the total. The majority no doubt exhibited Child's second type of adjustment, the *apathetic* reaction, in which the potential psychological conflict deriving from cultural duality is avoided by deemphasizing and "de-emotionalizing" the symbols and facts relating to nationality. Unlike the rebel, the apathetic individual takes his time Americanizing himself. He is likely to consider himself neither an Italian nor an American but rather, in keeping with the public image of him, an Italian American. The individual is apathetic only in the sense that he is not willing to take sides on the issue, raised by the rebel and the Americanists on the one hand and the old folk on the other, of whether one ought to try to be thoroughly American or to honor the institutions and ideals of his parents. His strategy is to quietly gain a certain degree of acceptance in both cultures by refusing to maintain any consistent nationality label.

If we characterize the rebel as a "status climber," the apathetic individual may instead be viewed as less impatient with the slow-paced changes in his status and in his nationality group. He moves at a relatively slow pace toward becoming completely assimilated to American society. By contrast, the rebel achieves this absorption rapidly. This speed is possible not only because he tries harder but also because he often marries outside the group, leaves the Italian community, Americanizes his name, makes every effort to control the telling aspects of his upbringing, and thus encounters fewer discriminations of the type suffered by most if not all ethnic groups during the first decades of their settlement.

There is a parallel here to what Norbert Wiley (1967) has termed "the ethnic mobility trap." Challenging the prevalent academic conception of a continuous stratum-like structure, Wiley proposes conceptualizing the opportunity structure in the form of a tree, with two kinds of social mobility. One route lies along the "trunk" all the way to the top. The other route is along one or the other of the "limbs" "leading gently upward but primarily outward" (Wiley, 1967:148). In a sense, the apathetic ethnic may be viewed as climbing slowly up a limb, together with the rest of his kind, until the limb possibly grows *up and into* the upper limbs that represent national society as a whole. The rebel by contrast leaves his ethnic limb to climb the main trunks of American society as an individual. His advancement to the top is direct and thus speedier.

There is a certain irony in all this. While still in the ethnic community, the rebel is usually at the bottom of the social hierarchy by virtue of his "anticipatory socialization" (Merton, 1957:265–268) for entrance into the larger society. But his departure from the community makes mobility more rapid. Given the proper talent and skill, mobility chances for ethnics are probably always best for those "at the bottom," namely, the rebels who deviate from the norms of their own group.

This is true for a variety of reasons. First of all, the rebel is often a man "driven" by a burning ambition. Second, he is among the first to take advantage of, if not create, the new institutional arrangements emerging in the larger society to accommodate the newly arrived. Third, and perhaps more important, the larger society views his rejection of his ethnic group as an admission of the "superiority" of the dominant group. He is thus likely to be seen as an intelligent, modern, "good boy," and is rewarded with opportunities to prove himself.

In a sense, the apathetic individual waits for his "foreignness" to fade away in the context of the educational, political, and economic achievements of his nationality group as a whole. Prejudice and discrimination are not emotionally serious problems for him. As he sees it, they either do not happen, or if they do, they are inevitable. Moreover, he feels that they are more likely to be triggered by class phenomena or political weakness than by ethnic characteristics. The apathetic individual is likely to have a circle of friends made up of members of his ethnic group, but some of his friends are from outside the group. If the latter are a minority, it is because they are more likely to live in different neighborhoods, and the apathetic individual has made no special attempt to reach out to them.

The girls these individuals go out with and marry are likely to be Italians, but this habit derives from residential proximity as much as from an individual preference resulting from socialization in the paternal family. As Child (1943:173) puts it, "they do not express any preference for Italian girls; they accept what is easy to get but do not attach any special value to it."

In short, unmotivated by the prospect of full and immediate assimilation into the larger society, and insulated to a considerable extent from it by residential segregation, the apathetic individual makes the transition from the parental culture to the new slowly, imperfectly, but with relatively little pain (Child, 1943:chap. 6). Caught as he is in this process of transformation, having no intention to fight it or accelerate it, he is "relatively unaware of differences between Italian and American cultures and on the whole even less aware of their significance in his own life" (Child, 1943:180). It follows that when the second generation is apathetic, intergenerational relations are likely to be characterized by mutual tolerance, or polite discord at the most.

The third type of reaction discussed by Child is that shown by the *in-grouper*. This individual resolves the conflict arising from contact with two mutually incompatible cultures by striving primarily for acceptance by the Italian group. Such individuals are no doubt in a minority, representing probably no more than 15–20 percent of the total second generation.

Child does not explicitly make the point; nevertheless, it appears that the in-grouper does not so much choose Italian culture over American culture but rather has a view of American society that is likely to be colored by the ethnic mosaic of the immigrant colony. For him, probably the most segregated of all Italian Americans, America is most readily visualized in terms of a division between Poles, Irish, Jews, Germans, Italians, and the like. He does not readily think of a national community in which these differences are somehow of secondary or little importance. Where he lives, the animosity between the various groups is intense—or in any case the memory of it is fresh. To turn inward, then, is not to reject American society and culture, but to assert the superiority of his nationality group over other nationality groups he encounters on the job or in the ghetto. This reaction represents a defensive hostility toward other nationality groups, a form of ethnocentrism induced by the interethnic clashes that, as we shall see, inevitably develop as various immigrant groups compete for space and jobs within the congested city. Child (1943:120) found among the in-groupers a "free enjoyment of Italian friends and Italian customs." Any one who attacked them with snide remarks or epithets was a good candidate for "a crack in the mouth."

Like self-conscious underdogs everywhere, in-groupers have a deep sense of being economically discriminated against and exhibit a marked degree of mutual identification. All efforts at group organization are admired. When Child did the study around 1940, many saw city politics as an avenue to Italian assertion and looked to an eventual Italian mayor through whom the Italians would "run the city."

All in-groupers prefer Italian girls as wives. In addition to being their own kind, Italian girls are "good" girls. As such, they may be expected not to disturb the husband's authoritarian and double-standard expectations concerning marriage. Many of the boys, however, prefer girls from other ethnic groups as mere dates because these are "more fun," while Italian girls tend to "get serious" too quickly.

At home, some cultural conflict arises, but by and large the second generation believes that the first can provide welcome advice about life and the world. The old folks are generally respected and loved. Their dialect is used frequently both at home and outside, where its use is considered a virtue in itself and sometimes a business advantage as well, considering the large size of the Italian population.

In short, when the in-grouper sees a conflict between his parents' culture and that of the larger society (in his own special image of it), he is likely to organize his behavior in such a way as to be in conformity with the former. He is keenly sensitive about possible disadvantages suffered by people of his kind not as individuals but as members of a group—"the Italians"—and he identifies strongly with the group. In a broader sense than that intended by Child, he is more nearly the real rebel—rebellious against what he sees as maltreatment of his people by other groups in the community. This attitude explains the emphasis on politics and the expectation of a coming Italian dominance in city politics. The in-group reaction offers the individual the chance to express the hostility that accompanies his striving for group status and is heightened by frustration of that striving (Child, 1943:chap. 5).

THE SECOND-GENERATION FAMILY. The third type of family considered by Campisi is the "second-generation" family. In this group both parents were either born in America of Italian immigrants or were brought over from the old country when they were still very young. They were the first to make the big cultural break between the old society and the new. Nevertheless, as previously noted, Child showed that the American-born children of immigrant parents have reacted differently to the clash between the two cultures. Consequently, one would expect to find variations within the second-generation family that reflect to some extent the types of reactions singled out by Child within the context of the first-generation family.

Campisi discusses three variations that correspond roughly to Child's three types of adaptation. One involves complete abandonment of the old world way of life in favor of thorough assimilation to American society. As Firey (1947:221) pointed out in his study of Boston, after they marry or soon thereafter, the couple tends to move away from the Italian neighborhood in search of more respectable localities in which to raise their children. Many change their Italian names and cease to use any form of the Italian language. Often, they have little to do with their foreign-born parents and relatives, visiting them only on such special occasions as Christmas, weddings, or funerals within the extended family group. This type parallels Child's "rebel" reaction. It comprises the rebel youngsters of the first-generation family who have married and gone their own way.

This group is a minority—almost certainly less than one-fourth of the entire second generation. A substantial percentage have gone to college. Hence, they are likely to have business, professional, and clerical jobs. They are manifestly mobile and highly ambitious people. Furthermore, they place a heavy emphasis on the importance of education, with the result that their children are almost invariably oriented toward obtaining a college education.

Little or nothing about these people may be labeled clearly "Italian American." In their eagerness to be thoroughly "American," many have married individuals from outside their ethnic group—frequently individuals who are themselves escaping ethnic identification. One spouse's desire and efforts to be "just a plain American" are thus reinforced by those of the other. As a result, with the possible exception of certain dietary habits acquired from the paternal family that are difficult to break but socially inconsequential owing to a certain cosmopolitan tendency in the American cuisine, there is little or nothing manifestly Italian in the rebel of the second-generation family.

Indeed, the rebels' most noteworthy characteristics are certain psychological and medical consequences of their almost pathetic efforts to sever all cultural ties with the world of the first generation. We have no data that touch directly on the Italian Americans, but studies of social stratification and mental illness have shown that sometimes the socially mobile must pay a great price in mental health for their strenuous efforts and their social exploits (Hollingshead and Redlich, 1958:368–370; Myers and Roberts, 1959:chap. 6; see also Bettelheim and Janowitz, 1964 for a review of literature). Mobility tends to loosen moral and social bonds, creating stress and various forms of self-destructive and anti-social behavior.

Very possibly, the price to be paid is especially steep among those who, in their efforts at individual achievement, have had to change name and religion; conceal their background or keep it inconspicuous; control the plethora of cultural and linguistic nuances that constantly threaten to break through and give them away; even sever all but the most superficial ties with the parental kin group. Among the rebels of the second-generation Italian American family, such behavior is common indeed, and one can confidently suggest that the incidence of mental illness among them is high.

A second form of the second-generation family, reflecting closely what Child termed the "apathetic" reaction, is no doubt the most frequent. The desire to become Americanized is perhaps as real as in the first form, but it is not combined with the rebel's impatience or the intensity of his negative attitudes toward the ways of the old folks. The parental culture is rejected as inapplicable, but not condemned. Consequently, though the family is likely to move away from the parental neighborhood and thereby lessen the frequency of communication with the first generation, the emotional bond with the old folks and their ways is not broken. Intimate communication is maintained with the parental household, and relations with all close relatives are marked by affection and understanding. The intimate interaction is, of course, facilitated by the Italian Americans' tendency to live in close proximity within the same city or in neighboring towns.

The practices and habits of this type of family are distinguishable as ethnic only upon close scrutiny. Except for a few simple phrases and words of Americanized dialect, the Italian language is largely unknown and is rarely if ever used with the young ones. On the other hand, the individual is not opposed to using what he knows, if the presence of the old folks demands it. When asked whether he speaks Italian, his answer is likely to be a relaxed and exaggerated yes—a fact that has led many social scientists to erroneously report that Italian is widely known in the Italian American community.

Their diet retains a certain residue of the Italian cuisine, especially on Sundays and holidays when various pasta and related meat dishes are quite regularly prepared by the vast majority of Italian American housewives. During the week, however, their culinary efforts are quite likely to resemble those of their non-Italian neighbors.

Given the physical proximity to large numbers of other Italian Americans, a large portion of their participation in primary groups is likely to take place among fellow Italian Americans of their own social class. Milton Gordon (1964:52) points out that in American society as a whole people tend to confine social participation in primary relationships to their own social class within their own ethnic group—that is, to the "ethclass."

Generally speaking, however, the family displays the behavior typical of the national social class to which it belongs. The bulk of its cultural and economic activities take place within the larger American community. Again Gordon (1964: 52) has argued that all people belonging to a social class are likely to act alike and to have similar values even if they have different ethnic backgrounds.

The vast majority of families of this type is found in the middle and working classes. Hence, the family is frequently characterized by child-centered attitudes on the part of the parents. Mother and father tend toward a democratic family pattern, and the father often shares the household duties, including the rearing of children, doing the dishes, and the like. When the children come of age, the selection of a marriage partner is exclusively their own affair. To an increasing degree, they choose members of other ethnic minorities and, less frequently, of other religions.

A third form taken by the second-generation family of Italian Americans is reminiscent of Child's "in-group" reaction. The couple prefers to remain in the Italian neighborhood close to the parental home and to the residences of the extended kin group. Such families may be found in the few remaining pockets of Italians that may properly be termed little Italies. However, as is often true of studies in the social disciplines, we know more about the exception than about the rule. Our knowledge of this type of family, which represents a small minority of Italians in America, is quite considerable in comparison to what we know about the second generation as a whole.

The Italian American families of the now demolished West End of Boston who were studied by Herbert Gans (1962) represent the type of family we are discussing. The study, carried out in the late 1950s, involved second-generation persons who were "mainly in their late thirties and forties . . . raising their own children." Gans (1962:18) proposed that West Enders were "almost, but not entirely, representative of the mainstream of second-generation Italian life in America," and the subtitle of his book is "Group and Class in the Life of Italian-Americans." This emphasis represents a gross and unfortunate misstatement. As Chapter 6 will show, on the basis of 1960 census data, second-generation Italian Americans equal or surpass the average native white in education, occupation, and income. As such, they are a far cry from the predominantly working class and lower class people Gans observed in the Boston ghetto.

Even the picture on the cover of Gans' book, which shows a manifestly underprivileged child of the slums, reveals the sampling restrictions of Gans' study. Indeed, Gans himself (1962:32, 122) states that his subjects were mostly working class and lower class people and that "Italians occupy a 'lower' position in the Boston labor market . . . than they do in New York, Chicago, and other large cities." More curious still is the fact that, although the body of Gans' book purports to be a study of "group and class in the life of Italian Americans," one late chapter (1962:chap. 11) states and cogently defends the thesis that the author's findings point to "a working-class phenomenon and that class differences separate the West Enders from the middle class."[1]

Despite the shortcomings of Gans' study, it will be useful to follow its discussion of the West Enders' family (Gans, 1962: chap. 3), for it suggests aspects of southern Italian culture that still linger among Italians in America. Gans finds that the second-generation family of the West Enders falls between the nuclear type, which includes only husband and his wife and children, and the extended type, in which a group of nuclear families and related individuals from several generations are united as a virtual unit. Distinguishing between household and family, Gans finds that households are generally nuclear although there is a certain tendency toward enlarging the circle of kin living under the same roof. For instance, married daughters often maintain close ties with their mothers by settling near them, a circumstance that makes it possible to find the two ladies in each other's company quite frequently. Nevertheless, the differences between the generations are large enough, and conflict therefore so likely, that mother and daughter do not share the same apartment.

Although the household is usually nuclear in character, the family is close to the extended type. However, while the classical extended family included a series of nuclear families functioning as an economic unit, the West End family is instead a "social circle." The social circle is a group "in which relatives who share the same interests, and who are otherwise compatible, enjoy each other's company."

It is clear that adaptation to American society and cultural estrangement from the old society occur even in this, an in-group type of family. Gans' finding that the extended family system is limited generationally supports this contention. Gans discovered that relationships between adults of the second generation and their parents, the immigrant generation, are fewer and less intimate than those between adults of the same generation, namely, between brothers, sisters, cousins, and the like. The old folks are visited, "but parents are generally not part of the continuing social life of the family circle." Moreover, the old people are freely criticized for such things as spoiling their grandchildren and "for insisting on outmoded ideas." Even when the tie between first and second generations is close, as it is in the example of the mother-daughter relationship, "mothers tend to assist rather than guide their married daughters."

In short, even in this type of family, which one would expect to exhibit the most interdependent features, the second generation has apparently achieved complete autonomy from the first. Furthermore, it appears that the close ties to the extended kin group are more a reflection of a lower class and working class phenomenon than an indication of sentimental attachment to a specific ethnic culture. Sociologists have accumulated evidence that the higher a person's social status in urban America the greater his participation in formally organized voluntary associations. Using this finding as a take-off point, Floyd Dotson (1951:687–693) interviewed fifty randomly selected families of skilled and semiskilled American-born workers from a working class district in New Haven to determine what forms of social organization they had developed for their leisure-time activities. He discovered that many families in the sample belonged to extended kin groups that constituted "nearly self-sufficient recreational" units. Specifically, Dotson found that in at least fifteen of the fifty families, the leisure time of the spouses was completely preempted by the activities of the kin group. In another twenty-eight families, regular visiting patterns with relatives constituted a major form of social activity.

Gans' study suggests that the husband-wife relationship in the West End is another area where the old cultural habits are tenacious insofar as it is reminiscent of the *segregated* marital relationship that is often observed in English, Italian, and other European families. Man and wife tend to have clearly distinct tasks and separate interests and activities. They have different leisure pursuits and separate circles of friends. A man's chief role is to bring home the pay check. The role of the wife, on the other hand, is much more varied. She is responsible for the rearing of the children (except for their discipline which is usually performed by the father after he comes home from work); she is also responsible for finding an apartment, keeping the house clean, and discharging most, if not all, the other housekeeping duties.

This type of relationship tends to produce and sustain a certain emotional distance between man and wife. Although West Enders seek out their marriage mates on the basis of the romantic love complex, in general there is little communication, conversational or otherwise, between husband and wife. Their mutual satisfaction derives almost exclusively from their sexual activity. When problems and troubles arise, they are more likely to take them to brothers, sisters, friends, and other relatives than to each other. The husband will talk them over with other men; the wife will talk with her sisters or mother.

This sort of affective segregation between the sexes is rather typical of working class couples in general (see Green,

1960:608–615; Bott, 1957:58 ff.; Rainwater, 1960:69). The phenomenon is probably tied to the lack of funds that would make it possible for the spouses to engage in recreational activities together, to the lack of inexpensive and proper recreational opportunities in the neighborhood, and to the street-corner mentality of the husband who as a youth grew accustomed to the company of the old gang of fellows gathered on the corner.

To some extent, the kind of emotional distance between marriage partners found by Gans is probably also a relic from the old society. In Italy the wife was constantly busy preparing food, watching over the children, putting them to bed, ministering to their health, sewing in preparation for her daughter's marriage, going to church, and the like. All these things she usually did at her home in the village. Her husband, on the other hand, was at work on the fields. When he came home late in the evening he was too tired to help with family matters, and he usually went to bed early so that he might arise before dawn and be out on the fields again by sunrise. On those very few occasions when he was not exhausted, he found it proper to join a few friends and relatives for a chat around the corner or for a game of cards and wine in the local tavern. As a result of these and other factors, there was very little affective communication between man and wife. The fact that they had been near-strangers to each other before their marriage did not help matters.

Looking at the phenomenon dynamically, Gans discerned signs of its eventual disappearance. In the first place, the change seemed to go hand in hand with an improvement in the educational and economic status of the family. In the second place, the change was associated with the disappearance from the neighborhood of the clubs that, organized by the immigrants for card playing and other forms of male socializing, tended to keep husbands away from home after work. The second generation showed no liking for these ethnic clubs. At the same time, the young people did not consider drinking at the local tavern an attractive way of spending time. There was an increasing tendency to gravitate toward home, with activities with the boys occupying perhaps one or two evenings a week. Naturally, the more time the men spent with their wives, the greater the likelihood that, given a normal degree of emotional compatibility, a feeling of fellowship developed between the two spouses.

Gans found that the West End family was an adult-centered family. Children were not the focus of the family life, as generally happens in the middle class. Instead, the household was run to satisfy adult wishes first. Gans (1962:56) noted:

> As soon as they are weaned and toilet-trained, they are expected to behave themselves in ways pleasing to adults. When they are with adults, they must act as the adults want them to act: to play quietly in a corner, or to show themselves off to other adults to demonstrate the physical and psychological virtues of their parents. Parents talk to them in an adult tone as soon as possible, and, once they have passed the stage of babyhood, will cease to play with them. When girls reach the age of seven or eight, they start assisting the mother, and become miniature mothers. Boys are given more freedom to roam, and, in that sense, are treated just like their fathers.

In their own world, children were given a high degree of autonomy, and parents gave them little or no guidance. According to Gans (1962:56–57),

> Parents are not expected to supervise, guide, or take part in it [the children's world]. In fact, parent-child relationships are segregated almost as much as male-female ones. The child will report on his peer group activities at home, but they are of relatively little interest to parents in an adult-centered family. If the child performs well at school or at play, parents will praise him for it. But they are unlikely to attend his performance in a school program or a baseball game in person. This is his life, not theirs.

West Enders allegedly were not particularly concerned with "developing" their children, in the sense of raising them to achieve a particular goal. West Enders did not worry much about such things as the future of their children, their occupational achievements, or their social status.

West Enders want for their children what they want for themselves—a secure existence as persons who are both accepted and somewhat envied members of their family circle and peer group. They hope that their children will seek a better education and obtain a better job than they, but the children are not pushed hard toward this goal. If a child does not achieve the parental wishes, he is pressed no further. Indeed, the parents' greatest fear is that the child will become a "bum." The worry about downward mobility is stronger than any desire for upward mobility. Consequently, the major hope is that in education, occupation, and general status, the child will not fall below that of his peers (Gans, 1962:60).

As in the case of their participation in voluntary associations, the behavior displayed by the West Enders in relation to their children is typical of all economically underprivileged people. Although a more detailed discussion of this theoretical problem must be deferred to Chapter 6, it can be stated here that such people do indeed dare hope for a better education and a better job for their children. At the same time they know how difficult it is for people in their position to achieve such goals. As a result, realists that they are, they do not push their children toward goals that for some are in the neighborhood of the impossible. The problem of achievement and motivation was succinctly stated by C. Wright Mills (1956:111) in his discussion of the economic psychology of "the very rich":

The accumulation of advantages at the very top parallels the vicious cycle of poverty at the very bottom. For the cycle of advantages includes psychological readiness as well as objective opportunities: just as the limitations of lower class and status position produce a lack of interest and a lack of self-confidence, so do objective opportunities of class and status produce interest in advancement and self-confidence.

The West Enders' adjustment to their way of life and their satisfaction with participation in the activities of the peer group helped prevent the development of a compelling need to achieve according to the standards of a middle class society. Having "a good time" by participating in such activities as chatting, bowling, and eating good food with one's friends and relatives was a real, immediate, and apparently satisfactory alternative to middle class ambition. In short, the lack of equal access to the means for high levels of economic, educational, and social achievement may undermine the resolve to strive because striving often meets with failure. But, as Gans (1962:252) properly noted, the movement from one social class or standard of living to another is a cultural change requiring not only access to the necessary means of achievement but also "the willingness and ability to accept them." West Enders were not particularly eager to accept these means. Thus if they effectively represented the many millions of Italians in America, we should expect to find a low level of achievement in this ethnic group. Chapter 6, however, demonstrates that, according to this logic the West Enders must have represented only a very small section of the Italians in America.

THE THIRD-GENERATION FAMILY. In 1948, Campisi did not even consider the third generation. (It hardly existed.) More than two decades later, it is necessary to at least mention it. The majority of Americans of Italian origin are not recorded by the census because they are members of the third and fourth generations. The children of most Italian immigrants achieved adulthood and started raising their own families in the late 1920s or early 1930s. The grandchildren, the third generation, in many cases now have their own families. Many no longer have Italian names. Damato is translated as Adams; Farnese as Farner; La Rocca as Stone or Roche; Ricci has become Ritchie; Lo Prete is sometimes Lopert; Lombardi is often Lombard; Pavone is translated by Peacock; Rossi is Ross; Gennaro has become January. Family names consisting of a combination of titles, Christian names, or attributes (like Boncompagni, Giancotta, Pietrantuono) have been shortened or translated; surnames ending in "i" have changed the "i" to a "y" or an "ie."

One encounters these "hidden" Italian Americans everywhere and in all walks of life. Generally speaking, however, they are members of the more prestigious occupations. They are college administrators, wealthy businessmen, and well-established professional men. Many of them are children of the second-generation "rebels," and they are sometimes off-spring of ethnic intermarriages. Almost invariably they themselves are married to members of other ethnic groups. Nothing or very little about them is identifiable as Italian.

Most third-generation individuals, however, still have Italian names and indeed are rather close, in both a physical and a cultural sense, to their parental family. What form of family organization do such people exhibit? Does it reveal anything peculiarly Italian? The temptation is to think that it does. A young sociologist writes from the State University of New York at Buffalo that he is carrying out a study to illustrate that third- and fourth-generation Italian Americans display definite Italian traits. Nevertheless, he notes:

> I am finding it most difficult to identify, isolate, and de-scribe these "Italian" traits, although I feel positive that they exist: for instance, family roles, "sentimentality," sexual roles ("good and bad" girls), etc.[2]

Chances are that there are indeed aspects of family behavior in the third generation that in some degree may be viewed as peculiarly Italian American. They are difficult to isolate, how-ever, because those aspects that they have in common with Americans in corresponding social classes in general out-number by far the idiosyncrasies.

In keeping with an American norm, the married third-generation Italian American man is likely to have a spouse who bears no resemblance to the old immigrant woman who considered herself entirely dedicated to her husband's wishes and caprices, and he accepts this behavior as proper. The third-generation woman, in turn, is married to a man who does not see himself as the absolute ruler of the family and the undisputed arbiter of all family affairs. Marital roles are divided along sex lines, but there are many areas—including child-rearing and discipline, cooking, cleaning—in which at times the two spouses exchange or complement roles.

The third-generation Italian American family finds the

general American pattern thoroughly congenial. A few vestiges from the past may remain, however. The majority of the third generation have had some cultural contact not only with their second-generation parents but with their grandparents, the immigrants, as well. Since many of the grandparents did not speak English fluently, the third generation had to learn some of their language, or at least develop a certain sensitivity in order to be able to communicate with them. Depending on the attitude of the parents, this circumstance has produced a "feeling" for the old-timers' culture. For instance, one sometimes observes a husband showing a certain over-protectiveness of his wife that echoes the grandfather's behavior after he realized that his old world wife was like a fish out of water in the new society.

The third-generation family is decidedly child-centered. The children are deliberately instructed in the ways of the American middle class. Education is highly valued. Indeed, in reaction to the lack of education in the family background, the parents are often obsessively concerned with the success of the children in school. However, given their current adherence to the Catholic religion and their physical concentration in urban areas characterized by school disorders, a disproportionate percentage of their children attend Catholic schools.

Third-generation individuals display one trait that is worth a brief note here though it does not specifically concern the family. Many of them exhibit a certain cultural "atavism." Such individuals probably exceed the number of in-groupers in the second generation, although they do not match their intensity of feeling. Now that they have "arrived" and are rarely if ever subjected to prejudice, the third generation individuals are much more secure about their ethnic background and sometimes eagerly manifest pride in it. This pride is expressed by talks of a future visit to Italy, an interest in Italian politics or literature, an admiration for Italian films and fashions.

Perhaps this reversal reflects a more general law of human behavior. In the initial stages of contact with the larger society, an ethnic group reacts to harsh efforts to socialize it with defensive behavior, which sometimes includes individual efforts to hide ethnic identity. But once recognition from the dominant group has been obtained, there is a symbolical return to the old culture, almost as if to redeem concessions of pride made in the initial stages.

In recent years, this phenomenon has been encouraged among the Italians of America by a resurgence of American interest in Italian institutions, by the recent popularity of Italian popular arts and fashions, and by the American tourist's selection of Italy as a favorite destination. Third-generation Italian Americans observe that their fellow members of the middle class have positive, even romantic, attitudes toward Italian society; hence they take pride in their cultural roots.

Religion

The family has traditionally been *the* core institution of Italian society and culture. Consequently, it has received heavy emphasis because its role is essential to an understanding of the adjustment of the Italian immigrant and his children to American society and culture. Next to the family, the Catholic religion has been the most critical institution for the Italians. Even so, its importance has been distinctly secondary to that of the family. To understand this fact, one must first understand the nature of religious life in the Italian South.

The people in southern Italy have never been pious. Barring special occasions—the Christmas and the Easter holidays plus various feasts of the patron saints and the many manifestations of the Virgin Mary—churches in the agricultural villages are quite likely to be empty. Religious services are customarily attended by a score of old ladies and spinsters and a handful of very old gentlemen working diligently toward salvation in view of their imminent Confrontation. Young and middle-aged males will go to church only on very special occasions. But even then they are likely to congregate outside the church and chat about various secular matters instead of attending the services inside.

exploitation

The religiosity of southern Italians is undermined by their relation to the priest. In the first place, the Catholic church has traditionally either exploited the peasants or sided with the large landowners in their exploitation of them. There were times and places in the South where the Catholic church owned as much as 75 percent of the local land. The figure of the priest, in whose person Christ is presumably reflected, was thus associated with the figure of the avaricious and cruel landlord. Were Catholicism a religion to emphasize man's direct relation to his god, such a conception of the priest might leave a man's religious feeling undamaged. But the Catholic church represents the priest as no less than the mediator between man and God—indeed, under certain circumstances he is an *alter Christus* (another Christ). The result is that a man's sense of distance from his priest is to some extent generalized to God himself.

Second, for a long time, in some places the priest was the only "educated" individual in the village. Isolated, lonesome, and bored, he did not find it particularly easy to have compassion and respect for his parishioners. When he did not exploit the peasants, he was likely to treat them with considerable haughtiness. Even when he displayed no obvious contempt for the humble peasant and his uneducated world view, he was likely to anger him by real or imagined amorous interests in his wife and daughter. In short, through the centuries, a chasm—spiritual, social, intellectual, economic—developed between the church, as represented by the local priest, and the working masses.

The preceding portrayal of the priest is at direct variance with one offered by Lawrence Pisani (1957:164), who argues that the Italian "small-town priest was revered by his parishioners as one of themselves" and "understood and loved his people." Nothing could be further from the truth. At least in southern Italy, although the typical priest has indeed had peasant kinsfolk, he has characteristically proceeded to take on the demeanor of the signorial class, with all the arrogance, desire for domination, and contempt for the people that this entails. As a result of this and of the contempt traditionally bred by familiarity, Italians, "the church's guardians," have long had a remarkable capacity to distinguish between the will of the Lord and the will attributed to Him by mortals, whatever their ecclesiastical title. The spiritual influence of the priest, therefore, was never great among the people who came to America. It was much easier to frighten the poor peasant into submission than to evoke his religious piety.

The peasant believed in God and the various saints. Indeed he readily availed himself of the church at critical periods of his life: birth, marriage, and death. But his private conception of religion was nevertheless heavily strewn with all sorts of beliefs in the forces of good and evil and included faith in various sorts of magical practices. At the heart of such beliefs and practices was the religious *festa,* which basically was a social occasion for merrymaking or an excuse for a special meal and a few hours off from hard work. The festival—this light-hearted expression of godliness—*was* religion for the masses. It gave a concrete indication of heaven. It was ever so joyful. It gave respite from the endless toil.

When the peasants came to America and settled in the ghettoes of the big cities, they found a church organization and culture that was totally outside their experience. In the words of Oscar Handlin (1951:135):

> Arriving toward the end of the century, they moved into residential districts that in most cities had formerly been occupied by the Irish. . . . They were Catholics, but the Catholic churches they found in the neighborhoods they occupied were Irish and not Italian—as different from what was familiar to the newcomers as the chapels of the Episcopalians or Methodists. They were not content, and sought to recapture the old authenticity. The result was a struggle, parish by parish, between the old Catholics and the new, a struggle that involved the nationality of the priest, the language to be used, the saints' days to be observed, and even the name of the church.

The Catholic church in America was then as now dominated by the Irish hierarchy, whose conception of religion was markedly different from the Italian version. Irish religiosity was accompanied by a fervor and a faith difficult for Italians to understand. The sight of grown men taking communion on Sunday and counting the beads of a rosary was shocking to the Italian man, accustomed as he was to thinking of religion as an activity for women and children. The Irish, moreover, tended to mix religion in America with politics in the old country. To be an Irish Catholic was not merely a question of pure religious faith. This status also had a political component; it involved being anti-Protestant, and anti-English particularly. Among Italians, religion and politics did not complement each other so well. Indeed, at least for the educated few and those who became active in the various political movements and the trade unions, the Catholic church was to the Italian immigrant as Protestantism and the English had been to the Irish. Many Italians in this country could not help but remember the church's opposition to Italian unification. For these reasons, the Italian Catholics in America felt overwhelmed and alienated by the Irish attitude.

Matters were made worse by the fact that the Irishman's conception of religion tended to undermine the Italian's special interest in the religious festivals and in the social occasions that they represented. Nothing about religion was more important to Italians than the *festa*. Without it, religion was cold, formal, and lacking significance. They fought hard for it, and eventually in many cases they either organized their own church or had their own way despite the Irish hierarchy's accusations of paganism. A study in 1938 (W.F.W.P.W.P.A., 1938:88–89) pointed out that the factor that distinguished the Italian religious life from that of other national minorities was its folk quality. The writers give descriptions of various religious festivals of New York, such as this one of the festival of Our Lady of Mount Carmel, held on June 16th.

On this occasion Little Italy becomes completely transformed. The streets are decorated with flags, banners and flowers. Beautifully illuminated multi-colored arches extend from sidewalk to sidewalk across the roadway. Innumerable stands with pastries, fruits, and souvenirs line the thoroughfares. Worshipers of all classes and ages mill about in dense, jostling crowds. Among the devout Ital-

ians who come to the sanctuary to pay homage to Our
Lady of Mount Carmel are many living in the remoter
parts of the city, and some even from neighboring states
who have journeyed here for this occasion. Many of them
bring huge, ornate candles to light at the altar. Others
bring offerings of gold and silver plaques to the church
as tokens of gratitude for favors received at the hands of
the Blessed Virgin.

Such festivals exist even today in the few ghetto areas
where the immigrants and the in-groupers of the second generation continue to live. But they lack the pageantry and the
intense carnival atmosphere of years gone by. Moreover, as
the old-timers grow old and die, the festivals no longer per-
form their previous function. The southern Italian peasantry
traditionally had few or no public recreational facilities.
Church festivals filled this gap, in the Old World and, for a
while, in the New World as well. In American society, however, there never has been a scarcity of public recreational
opportunities. As the immigrants' children grew up, they took
advantage of public recreation, all the more so because it
aided in the process of cultural adaptation. The colorful
religious festivals thus gradually began to disappear.

In the church as in the family, "intergenerational" conflict
inevitably developed. If the old-timers felt the church in
America was not old-fashioned enough—in the sense that it
did not devote itself fully to maintaining the colorful folk
rituals of old—the new generations viewed it as "backward"
and tainted by superstition. Such divergent values created
grave problems of adjustment for the church. If it attempted
to reach the old folks by cultivating an atmosphere reminiscent of old times, the younger generation was estranged,
tending to regard the church as "foreign" and lacking in
sobriety. If the church sought to reflect urban realities and
organize itself along lines that were suitable to the new generation, the old folks stayed away. Time and the capacity for
compromise eventually solved the dilemma. The ultimate
success of the Catholic church among the Italians in America
owes much to its capacity to abandon those characteristically
Italian practices that in the eyes of the younger generation

marked it as "foreign" while at the same time retaining enough of the old atmosphere to make the old people feel that the church belonged to them.

Since the 1930s, there has been no "religious problem" to speak of. Indeed, as the Italians have adapted themselves to American society, the Catholic church has succeeded not only in winning their loyalty but also in gaining their respect. Nelli (1967:49) considers 1945 the year in which the Catholic church assumed a position of social importance among the Italians in America. That occurrence, it might be added, roughly marks the beginning of the final stage of their social assimilation. Religiosity is often a symbol of social respectability. In Italy, religious participation is predominantly a characteristic of the poor and the lowly. In America, it is an important sign of social propriety in the working and middle classes. In keeping with national criteria of social respectability, Italian Americans have found that membership in the ethnically mixed Roman Catholic church of the suburbs is an important expression of their new middle class status. Moreover, the rising Italian middle class that adopts American Roman Catholicism as a token of its new status adopts the parochial school as an equivalent symbol. As Nathan Glazer and Daniel Moynihan (1963:202–203) point out "in the third generation, the influence of Catholicism among Italian Americans has become formidable . . . the student body of Fordham University, for example, has become half Italian." There is a degree of irony in all this. The Italians, for two thousand years the chief trustees of Roman Catholicism, have adopted in America a form of Catholicism that socially and ritually bears little resemblance to what they knew in Italy, illustrating once again the drive toward assimilation generated in ethnic groups by American society.

Italians are no longer greatly concerned that their churches be run by Italian priests. In any case the desire was never realistic, for the Italians do not now (and never did) provide enough priests. Instead, the Italians join in prayer their Polish, German, and, especially, Irish co-religionists and send their children to the same schools. It is in school and in church that the melting pot is beginning effectively to do its work. As Glazer and Moynihan (1963:204) observed, "The Irish and Italians, who often contended with each other in the city, may work together and with other groups in the Church in the suburbs, and their separate ethnic identities are gradually being muted in the common identity of American Catholicism."

The Italians' tradition of secularism and skepticism toward church authority, however, has not disappeared and remains ingrained in the younger generations of the suburbs. Superficially, religious beliefs and practices seem to differ little between Irish Americans and Italian Americans. Closer scrutiny, however, reveals certain distinctive attitudes and beliefs. Nothing indicates the difference between the two groups more effectively than their respective stands on the use of contraceptive devices—an issue that has generated stormy dialogue within the Roman Catholic church in recent years. In late 1965 a national survey showed that only 37 percent of wives who came from Irish families used artificial means of contraception and thereby flouted church authority. By contrast, 68 percent of wives from Italian backgrounds used such means, showing thereby a higher degree of independence from the church in one of the most sacred areas of its doctrine (Potvin *et al.*, 1968).[3]

The Padrone *Complex*

The evolution of the family among Italians in America and to a lesser extent their changing participation in the religious life illuminate the problems they have had to solve in the process of Americanization. In conclusion, one other significant aspect of their experience should be mentioned.

In the early days of the Italian immigration, when the immigrants were employed almost exclusively as railroad laborers and construction workers, they frequently worked in work gangs supervised by individuals known as *padroni*, or by the *padroni's* representatives. These individuals often had contracts with employers to supply them with squads of laborers, and in this capacity they had ample opportunity to abuse their fellow countrymen.

It is generally believed that the "*padrone* system" was imported from Italy. In an interesting paper, Marie Lipari (1935) took issue with this position, arguing that the general economic structure of the United States was responsible for the existence and growth of America's version of this ruinous phenomenon. She found precedents in the colonial practice of apprenticeship and indentured service and in the practice of peonage, which began in the South after the Civil War.

With the great expansion of American industry and commerce, employers were forced to depend more heavily than ever before on immigrant labor, a circumstance that is reflected in a law passed by Congress in 1864. The law, repealed in 1868, legalized all contracts made in foreign countries by prospective migrants to the United States, in which the migrants pledged their services to someone in the United States for no longer than twelve months, in order to assure repayment of passage advanced them by the sponsor (known among Italian immigrants as the *padrone*).

Employers who needed labor often found it convenient to turn to an individual—sometimes an employee who had demonstrated linguistic skills and qualities of leadership—for assistance in locating manpower. This "labor agent," or *padrone*, went abroad to find the needed labor or commissioned others abroad to find recruits. In time, he began to work independently of the employers and became a "businessman" in his own right.

In his popular account of Italians in America, Michael Musmanno (1965:91) threw light on the *padrone* phenomenon by launching into the fictitious story of a typical young Italian immigrant. Antonio, as Musmanno calls him, is able to pay for the passage to America because he enters into an agreement with an Italian from the United States, the *padrone*. Visiting Antonio on his farm, the *padrone* offers to advance one-half of the passage money, provided that Antonio agrees to repay him with interest after starting work on the job the *padrone* will find for him. When Antonio arrives in America, the *padrone* in fact finds him a job.

The hours would be from six in the morning until six in the evening, and the wages one dollar a day, from which would be deducted the cost of maintenance and, at intervals, a certain other amount until the *padrone* had been reimbursed (with interest) for the sums he had expended.

The *padrone* was relatively free to handle the workers as he wished. The possibilities of exploitation were legion. To begin with, the amount he charged the immigrant for his passage was sometimes several times the actual fare. Second, he made handsome profits by boarding newly arrived immigrants at exorbitant prices until they were sent to their jobs. Third, the *padrone* charged the immigrant a fee, called *bossatura*, for finding him employment, and this fee amounted to from one to ten dollars. Fourth, the job was sometimes located in a distant location, and the immigrant could thus be charged extravagant fees for transportation and for a place to sleep. Finally, once he had his job, the worker was forced to buy from a store run by the *padrone,* where the prices were fixed at the *padrone*'s convenience.

It is difficult to determine accurately how many Italian immigrants were, at one time or another, under the influence of the *padrone* arrangement. One source estimated in 1897 that two-thirds of the Italian male population of New York and adjoining municipalities were affected by it (Koren, 1897:122). In any case, a very large number of immigrants took years paying debts accumulated through the machinations of the clever *padroni,* and this greatly retarded their adjustment to and effective participation in American society.

Various agents tried to break up the *padrone* system and improve the conditions of the unfortunate workers. For a while at least, these efforts failed because of the ignorance of the workers, their fear of the *padroni* and the "strange characters" who were their supporters, lack of cooperation on the part of the employers, and downright resistance on the part of Italian American *prominenti* (leaders), who often had been themselves *padroni.*

Failure to quickly eradicate the evil was probably due also to the reluctance of the immigrants to be organized by the labor movement. Edwin Fenton (1957:30) finds that the masses of Italian immigrants played a small role in the labor movement of the United States. According to him, "They were village-minded, fatalistic, and self-reliant, three qualities which made them poor labor union members."

The early Italian immigrants earned their reputation as poor labor union material for two basic reasons. In the first place, they accepted wages that were considered too low by organized labor and by the labor force already established in their area. The acceptance of low wages by such large numbers of people, it was feared, drove general wages down—or at least kept them from rising at an acceptable pace—and hindered the move for better working conditions. The charge was inevitable. Workers in a given area are always alarmed when a new and sizable work force appears among them. If, however, the economy is healthy and vigorous, as the American economy generally was fifty to seventy years ago, the new labor force further stimulates production, resulting in better wages and improved working conditions for all workers in the area.

In any case, most Italian immigrants failed to appreciate the benefits of union membership because they believed they would be in this country only temporarily. Hence they had neither the time nor the patience to engage in such union practices as strikes or even absenteeism from work, activities that have notoriously long-range effects. But even if they desired to engage in union-approved work practices, their virtual bondage to the corrupt *padroni* and their capitalist clientele would have prevented them.

The Italians were also considered poor union material because early Italian immigrants were sometimes used as strike breakers. Given their poverty and their reliance upon the *padroni* for a job, again they had little or no choice. Furthermore, since they depended on the *padroni*'s transportation to the job, the Italian laborers did not always know that they were being sent to work in struck plants (Pisani, 1957:92).

It is also worth noting that the newly arrived Italian laborers were rarely if ever welcome in the existing unions. It is a rare working man who has an abstract view of the consequences of universal unionization. Students of social classes may—and indeed invariably do—see the process of enlarging the union fold as beneficial to the working class as a whole. A particular group of workers, however, will often see their union as a "private reserve," an instrument of their particular interests that is likely to lose its effectiveness if it does not remain closed to outsiders.

Today, American workers of Italian background are active in the labor unions of the country, and many of them are leaders at the local, regional, or national level. As the immigrants and their descendants cast their lot with America and adapted themselves to American conditions, they were eager candidates for union membership, and the unions welcomed them. The motives that drove the early immigrants to "make a fast buck" and leave have now disappeared, and the Italians now see the union as the chief safeguard against possible encroachments on what they conceive as their fair share of the national wealth. Italian Americans today are very powerful in some unions. Ironically, in their new position of privilege, they have joined older ethnic groups in barring from membership those who today are repeating, to some extent, their earlier experience, notably the Black Americans, the Puerto Ricans, the Mexican Americans, and various small groups of new arrivals.

This chapter has shown that, when they first arrived, and for several decades afterwards, Italian immigrants had a trying time. Impoverished, ignorant, and bewildered, they fell easy prey to those, like the *padroni,* who wanted to enrich themselves at the immigrants' expense. Their progress toward Americanization was retarded. In the meantime, the efforts of others to change their very conception of god and religion resulted in a compromise. However, the immigrants' children and grandchildren, with a keen eye to religion as a social institution, now appear to be winning over the old folks in the matter of religious practice in a way that the Irish could not win several decades ago. The Italian immigrants, and their children for that matter, have also had to adapt their ways even within the context of the family, the most sacred of their institutions. Intergenerational relations have not been smooth. Nevertheless, they were never so stormy as other types of relationships to which we shall now turn.

Notes

[1] There is another, very important issue on which Gans and various other American writers (see Rosen, 1959; Strodtbeck, 1958) must be taken to task in the hope that certain errors of a historical and methodological nature may be avoided in the future. In studying Italians in America, they often find it useful to consider the possible roots of their behavior, and tend to find such roots in Italian society as it was prior to the great emigration. In itself that is an honorable procedure. But failing to consider the facts of Italian social history, they perpetuate the most improbable myths—myths that originated in the lifeless little schemes of researchers and the uncritical minds of those who would generalize the personal experience of a single immigrant (the "informant") to a goodly portion or all of Italian society. Consider, for instance, the following fantasies found among innumerable others in Gans' book (1962, chap. 10): the social and economic conditions that existed in the Italian South at the turn of the century "still hold today"; southern Italian parents "had little interest" in their children "as individuals, except to show them off"; all people outside the family circle of relatives "were conceived to be strangers" and "only relatives were invited into the home" (Gans would find even today that the people of rural southern Italy shut their doors only at night and that neighbors move about freely in each other's houses, whether they are relatives or not); people from other communities, even near-by ones, "were characterized as criminals"—no doubt a "fact" revealed by a single immigrant on the basis of his own personal view of things in a single southern Italian village; women were almost completely dependent on men because, among other things, "they could not work as laborers, and no other jobs existed" (this makes one wonder what happened to olive and grape pickers, wheat cutters and carriers, weeders, fruit pickers, and many such others, all of which are traditionally female occupations).

Curiously, too, some writers seem oblivious of the possibility that much of Italian American behavior has roots nowhere but in the American slum. Gans (1962:83) found that native-born West Enders were unconcerned about saving and that, indeed, they criticized "recent Italian immigrants . . . who saved their money to buy a home after living only a few years in America." Again he (Gans, 1962:256) observed that, among West Enders, as among other ethnic groups, many immigrants who came to America as children were socially mobile and tended to be leaders. Gans' explanation—and a reasonable one, I might add— is that such individuals were not complete captives of the ambition-inhibiting "peer group society." Should such facts not have led Gans to consider the possibility that the will to success is powerful enough in the old country but is weakened or destroyed in the immigrant's child by the conditions of the American slum? They should, in any case, have sufficed to indicate that there are no purely Italian causes of behavior once Italian immigrants have crossed the ocean.

[2] Correspondence from John Andreozzi, November 10, 1968.

[3] This shows again how unrepresentative Gans' West Enders were. Gans (1962:54) found that "in the West End, children come because marriage and God bring them." The national survey shows that Italian Americans as a whole exhibit entirely different behavior.

Chapter 5 ◉ Intergroup Relations

The changes that occur in an immigrant group's language, religion, family organization, and so on represent one aspect of the assimilation process. The manner in which the group relates to others is another important aspect. Accordingly, this chapter concerns such phenomena as social acceptance or rejection, interethnic competition for jobs and space, intermarriage, and certain "pathological" responses, like crime, when these can be viewed as group reactions.

Most immigrants face problems of adjustment that can best be understood in terms of contacts between groups rather than between individuals. This condition is particularly evident in the United States, a country whose ethnic composition has regularly been in a state of flux. Competition for opportunities in an environment of unrelenting and profound social change inevitably has created major difficulties in intergroup relations.

By and large, the difficulties encountered by a newly arrived ethnic group vary in direct proportion to its *size*, the *rapidity* of its arrival, and its *cultural remoteness* with respect to other groups in general and to what might be termed the dominant group in particular. On all three counts, the Italians came to the New World almost predestined for serious trouble.

In the case of the Italian Americans intergroup relations may be conveniently divided into three major types. One type includes relations among the Italians themselves—it can logically be treated here because a deep cultural cleavage between northerners and southerners existed at the time of the great immigration. A second type pertains to the Italians' relations with other immigrant groups present in the immediate area and milieu of adjustment and acculturation. The third includes the Italians' relations to the larger society.

Group Relations Among Italians

As previously noted, the people of Italy constitute a cultural mosaic in their own right. The endless procession of armies that invaded the Italian peninsula through the centuries left their mark, in varying degrees and in different areas of the country, on the culture, language, and physical traits of its inhabitants.

When the Italians came to the United States, their differences were still fresh and unmitigated by the mixed marriages and cultural syncretism that have accompanied the recent massive internal migration taking place within Italy. As Carlo Golino (1959:21) notes, the Italian mass migration to the United States began a mere ten years after national unification and reached its climax when the first generation of Italian citizens had barely reached adulthood. Hence, the migrants left Italy not as Italians but as Genoese, Venetians, Neapolitans, Sicilians, Calabrians, and the like, and continued to identify themselves as such for some time, if not for the rest of their lives.

It would be too time-consuming to treat all these regional differences in detail, but much can be gained by considering only the chief geographical division, that between North and South. Today, many a scholar discussing cultural, economic, political, and social conditions in Italy will not hesitate to speak of "the two Italies." Toward the end of the nineteenth century, at the time of the great emigration, the expression was a great deal more valid than it is today.

The history of the North, more than that of the South, is a history of contact with the peoples of northern Europe. The immigrants from northern Italy, consequently, showed the cultural and physical characteristics of the older American stock more frequently than their southern fellows. This circumstance made them less suspect, less foreign, and hence more readily acceptable to the "old American" group. Their greater acceptability, in turn, reinforced in them an old feeling of superiority in relation to the southerners. Old geographical terms were translated into English and given social connotations. The people from the North, namely, *Alta Italia* (high or upper Italy) came to be known as "high Italians," while the people from the South, or *Bassa Italia* (lower Italy) were known as "low Italians." The ill repute in which the southerners were initially held in the new society gave the northerners cause to feel superior to them and to proclaim whenever necessary their distinctness from them. To reduce a very complex problem to a simple metaphor, the northerners were ever alert to avoid guilt by association.

The fact that the birth of the Italian nation was brought about largely by northerners (to be sure, it was mostly the work of the Piedmontese who did not emigrate in considerable numbers), while southerners took a rather passive role, gave the northerners further reason for pride and a sense of superiority. Finally, although other factors might be mentioned, the people from the northern regions could boast that their home contained the leading centers of Italian civilization. Had not the Genoese, who were the first to migrate to America, been preceded by their illustrious compatriot, Christopher Columbus? Other northerners had had their Dante, their Michelangelo, or their Rossini. Indeed, if the people of Latium may be included among the northerners, they also had the national capital with all its past glories.

The cultural heroes of the Italian South were more modest and less numerous, unless one went back to the Greek era. But that period was too remote to be significant in the social and intellectual conscience of the Italians. In short, the people of the North felt richer in tradition and culture, more civilized, closer to the loci of true "Italianity." In their eagerness to be accepted in American society, they declined to be identified with the "troublesome and ignorant" "Africans" of the South. For a time, a social chasm separated the peoples of the "two Italies," breeding substantial resentment and conflict.

There were other, more tangible, reasons why the northerners felt superior. As previously observed, Italian immigrants in general were poor, unschooled, and unskilled. The northerners, however, were better off than the southerners. For example, between 1899 and 1910, 77 percent of those who came from the South were farm workers or laborers; less than .5 percent were in the professions. By contrast, three times as many from the North were professionals, and 66 percent were farm workers or laborers. More telling still: only 11.5 percent of the northern immigrants were illiterate. The corresponding figure for the southerners was a stunning 53.9 percent. Finally, on arrival the northerners had on the average twice as much money as the southerners (A.R.I.C., 1911:97). To be sure, these differences were not really enormous, but they were big enough to produce a certain difference in class position between the two groups, and thus a degree of social distance and some divergences in interests and ideas. The differences also gave the immigrants from the North a significant margin in their adjustment to the new society.

That margin was increased by another factor. It will be remembered that the northerners were the pioneers of the Italian migration to the United States. Half a generation or more separated many of these first immigrants from the southerners who followed them. The northerners thus had a head start in the process of adjustment to the political, economic, and educational institutions of the new society. Caroline Ware (1935:152–153) pointed out that by the time of the southern immigration, the Genoese of Greenwich Village, who had come with an early contingent the bulk of whom had gone to California, had already established themselves in positions from which they could "look down with scorn upon the 'low' Italians." They also "could take pains neither to know nor to be classed with them, and could dominate the affairs of the Italian community from a lofty distance."

The cleavage between North and South was the worst division, but it is important to recognize that Italian immigrants were also divided, and so remained for some time, along numerous regional or provincial lines. The rugged Italian terrain, the poor system of communication in the nation's early days, and the tradition of serfdom that kept the peasant tied to a particular place, produced in the Italian countryside a peculiar phenomenon known as *campanilismo*. Deriving from the word *campana* (bell) and *campanile* (church tower), *campanilismo* refers to a view of the world that includes reluctance to extend social, cultural, and economic contacts beyond points from which the parish or village bell could still be heard. In short, it suggests a marked tendency among the Italians of sixty or more years ago to move and act in very narrow social circles. Even today in many Italian towns the term *forestiero* is used to refer to a person who may come from no further than the next village, scarcely two or three miles away, but who may nevertheless be viewed as alien, as complicated, inscrutable, and uncultivated as a *foresta* (forest).

Campanilismo was fostered by a variety of factors besides those already mentioned. In the first place, physical separation and lack of geographical mobility produced in each town a certain fossilization of culture. At the same time the custom and language of individual towns gradually became differentiated from each other. Even today in southern Italy, one need travel the mile or two that separates one village from another to find clear distinctions in linguistic forms and cultural content.

In the second place, *campanilismo* and the accompanying cultural antipathies relate to a phenomenon isolated by Karl Marx in his discussion of the class struggle. Marx argued that in their intense economic and political competition, "capitalists" often had to call upon the workers to help them combat other capitalists, in effect leading the workers to fight "the enemies of their enemies" and one another. Likewise, much of the inter-village strife that till recent times characterized southern Italy especially was a partial consequence of the competition and animosity that in times gone by had existed among the local land barons.

When the Italians came to the United States they imported a pitiful tendency to mistrust and avoid all those who did not share their particular dialect and customs. As a result, collective approaches to the problems created by their uprooting and by the necessity of adjusting to the new society tended to be organized along village lines, or at best on the basis of provincial (county) and regional (state) identification. Not surprisingly, Ware (1935:155) found that such social organizations as clubs and mutual benefit societies "were formed on the basis of the part of Italy from which people had come." Likewise, "informal social relations . . . were almost wholly restricted to people from the same town or province."

The provincial differences naturally were strongest during the initial period of the southerners' settlement in the New World, and in time they lost relevance or bite. Today they are hardly more than a memory among the few surviving old-timers. Their waning is due to various factors. First, as the immigrants learned the ways of the new society and began thinking of themselves as Americans, their previous differences naturally became less important; ironically, they tolerated each other better as fellow Americans than as fellow Italians. Second, their differences tended to fade as the inflow of new immigrants, bringing fresh reminders of cultural distinction, was greatly reduced, first by World War I, and then by the official immigration restrictions. Third, in the new society, new interests—for example, occupational trade and common politics—developed that cut across old lines. Fourth, the animus and the rejection that confronted all immigrants from the Italian South tended to produce a certain mutual sympathy, a consciousness of kind, a newly found sense of belonging together. Fifth, sheer physical contact or proximity, made inevitable by the nature of the little Italies, forced a certain mutual adaptation among the inhabitants, however great may have been the initial cultural distance. After all, they were now on the same block, often in the same building, and they had to learn to live with one another and practice a degree of give and take of one another. The sixth and most important factor is indirectly related to the first. To the children—American born or very young immigrants—the old world differences, suspicions, and animosities usually became irrelevant. They were concerned with the conditions that confronted them in school or on the job as second-generation Italian Americans rather than as Neapolitans, Sicilians, Genoese, and the like. On the street corner, the Irish gang engaged them in a fight as Italians not as individuals from particular regions of Italy. As many began to assign more importance to their role as Italian-Americans, to a lesser but appreciable extent their parents followed suit.

But what were the consequences of the initial differences and cleavages? These disagreements had a most important impact on the Italians' ability to achieve the primary goal of any immigrant group intent upon finding an honorable place within the host society: *political power*. It may be enunciated as a general principle that the greater the cultural cohesion of a subgroup in a society, the greater the likelihood that it will pursue common political action and the greater its success in achieving goals that are highly valued in the society.

In this respect, the Italians in America have had substantial but rather slow success. Although the apolitical tradition and poverty of their old world background are partly responsible for their slow political achievement, in large measure it is due also to their failure to engage in common action toward common goals once they reached America. Ware (1935:166) quotes one of the Italian politicians in Greenwich Village to the effect that "If the Italians stuck like the Jews, they would have half the city government by now." This may be an exaggeration, but it forcefully conveys the idea that poor cohesion existed in the Italian American community.

Glazer and Moynihan (1963:194) point out that in 1910 there were no less than 2,000 Italian mutual benefit societies in New York City—a fact that clearly indicates a high degree of fragmentation within the Italian community. To be sure, many of those societies were technically organized under the National Order of the Sons of Italy. But the order never became an effective national organization. Italian Americans have never had anything resembling B'nai B'rith or the American Jewish Committee. It is revealing that when, in 1961, Italian Americans wanted to protest against "The Untouchables," a television program they apparently felt was offensive because it concentrated on Italian-led crime rings, the Italians had to *create* a protest organization.

Today, the immigrant lodges, orders, and fraternal organizations are all but extinct. A very small percentage of men of the first and second generations do belong to such associations as Sons of Italy, Knights of Columbus, Unico Club, and Dante Alighieri Society. But it is hard to uncover the specific purposes and functions of such organizations. One gets the feeling that Italian Americans have their exclusive societies because other ethnic groups have theirs—because it is the thing to do. Also, they may fear the possibility that by virtue of their organization the other groups will reap advantages at the expense of the Italians. Organization thus represents, in some very vague sense, a precautionary measure necessitated by the power game being played by various ethnic interest groups.

Generally speaking, cooperative ethnic activity comes hard to Italian Americans. This deficiency is no doubt an inheritance from Italian society. The vicissitudes of their history produced among Italians an extreme degree of individualism that is controlled effectively only by the family group. The family is the only aggregate that they traditionally have been able to trust. Thus when they engage in extra-familial group activity, each is likely to be happy with nothing less than the leadership of the group. They will trust no one else. Everyone else is suspected of having an ulterior motive for wishing to lead or even join the group. Gans' (1962:106–110) West Enders were too late in their efforts to prevent the planned redevelopment of their district. But when they finally organized a Save the West End Committee, the group was ineffective because, as the old expression goes, there were "too many chiefs and no Indians."

It may be inferred from the preceding discussion that Italian Americans have little or no consciousness of kind, little or no pride in Italian culture and society. True, conversing about Italy with the old-timers, one is sometimes treated to nostalgic, even romantic, recollections. In most cases, however, a little probing will quickly elicit stories of great suffering and humiliation, and thus betray a deep resentment against a society that had no room for them and heaped all manner of scorn and afflictions on them.

The second generation takes an even more negative view of Italian society and culture. One reason, which has already been indirectly introduced, concerns a tendency to generalize their lack of respect for their parents—the "greasers"—to the Old World from which they came. Also important is the fact that the parents often referred to conditions in the old society as a way of emphasizing to their growing children how much better life was in America and how comparatively unruly the new generation was. In the process, most youngsters learned to like the old society even less than they respected their parents.

Such facts may explain why Italian Americans have made few efforts to provoke an interest in studies of Italian culture. When the second generation was growing up, some effort was successfully made to introduce the study of the Italian language into the high school curriculum. But this aim basically reflected utilitarian motives—the old-timers sought to be reinforced in their linguistic habits at home. In the early 1960s Professor Vincent Ilardi, a historian at the University of Massachusetts, attempted to interest various Italian American organizations in instituting a chair of Italian studies in one of the American universities that already possessed appropriate library facilities. His efforts came to nothing then, and for all I know they are fruitless still.

Perhaps the new interest in Italian culture displayed by some members of the third and later generations may soon improve matters in this respect, particularly since these Italian Americans have achieved respectable levels of education and economic affluence. Their interest, however, may be fleeting, and in any case it probably affects a minority of Italian Americans.

Although in the short run the lack of cohesion and consciousness of kind among Italian Americans seems to have prevented spectacular achievements for the group as a whole, in the long run it probably will produce a high level of assimilation in the national life. As Glazer and Moynihan (1963:216) have pointed out in the case of New York City, Italian Americans are rapidly moving toward a middle class style of life "which is American Catholic more than it is anything that may be called American Italian." In the process, sentimental ties to Italian culture are likely to be weakened rather than strengthened.

Interethnic Relations

An old sociological proposition that springs from the social psychology of rural America suggests that close physical proximity (for example, living in the same neighborhood) usually goes hand in hand with close interaction and hence intimate association, a "common spirit," a sense of "weness," as Charles H. Cooley (1909:23) put it. According to this scholar, the neighborhood and other "primary groups," like the family and the play group, are so important in creating and sustaining "a common whole" that they are basic in the formation of the very "social nature and ideals of the individual." Properly amplified to account for such factors as *equality* in interaction, *freedom* to leave the group, the *cost* of the departure, and the *alternatives available* for group life, the proposition appears to have some validity even today.[1] Interethnic contact, however, presents a situation that fails to support the proposition—sometimes for long periods of time.

The area of the city where Italians, Irish, Jews, and other ethnic groups lived close together was no neighborhood at all in the Cooleyan sense of the word. To use the title of a recent volume on ethnic relations, these people saw each other as the "strangers next door" (Robin Williams, 1964). The Italians who arrived in urban America from the ancient hills overlooking the Odyssean Mediterranean were not ready to include in a common whole their foreign neighbors, and this reluctance was readily reciprocated. As Ware (1935:83) noted in her study of Italians in Greenwich Village, "The new element which intruded into the block found no neighborhood group ready to absorb it, but rather a population, economically and socially distant, indifferent or hostile to the newcomers' arrival."

THE IRISH AND THE ITALIANS. Of all the ethnic groups that the Italians came in contact with the Irish were of special importance. It was with the Irish, their immediate predecessors in the procession of immigrant groups, that the Italians clashed most bitterly. The first conflicts between the two groups were primarily in the arena of economic interests. To the Irish, the Italians were foreigners and "dirty guineas" who invaded their neighborhood, stimulated its further deterioration, and then took it away from them. Moreover, because the Italians were often non-union laborers they sometimes took Irish jobs away or undermined the level of their wages.

In 1939 William Foote Whyte (1939:623–642) examined the stages of conflict resulting from contact between the Italians and the Irish in Boston's North End. Whyte discussed the period from 1860 to 1939, "during which the Italian population first challenged, then successfully rivaled, and eventually superseded the dominant Irish group" (Whyte, 1939:623).

The North End was predominantly Irish until 1880, when their proportion began to decline rapidly. Fifteen years later, the state census listed 7,700 Italians, 6,800 Irish, 6,200 Jews (predominantly Russian), 1,200 English (English, Scots, or Canadians), and 800 Portuguese. Through the years, the Italians continued to move in, while the Irish and other ethnics moved out, until at the time of Whyte's article, about 95 percent of the North End population was of Italian stock.

The Irish considered the Italians foreign intruders. Moreover, the Italians were viewed as menacing Irish jobs. In addition, many Italian immigrants depended on the *padroni* for getting work; hence, they could be—and in many cases were—used to undercut the wages paid to the Irish. The Irish, most of whom had come here to stay, also resented the Italians' obvious orientation toward the old community in Italy, where most intended eventually to return. As a result, their standard of living was low, for much of their income was sent to Italy, and their zeal for assimilation in American society left something to be desired. "While the Italians professed the same religion, their language, customs, and dress were incomprehensible to the Irish" (Whyte, 1939:625). They even seemed to enjoy their foreignness. Such attitudes angered the Irish and strengthened, for a while at least, their feelings of superiority and contempt for the Italians.

In the early days of the Italian immigration young Irishmen had a custom of hanging around barrooms and street corners. They looked upon certain strategic corners as their personal property. "If they did not like the looks or actions of trespassers, they felt that they had a right to take affairs in their own hands" (Whyte, 1939:626). Consequently, hostility between the Italians and the Irish took on the character of a struggle for personal security. For the early Genoese settlers it was dangerous to venture outside the small Italian settlement. A few of the tougher Irish would hang around the Italian area and "rob drunks or take money from Italians as they came home from work" (Whyte, 1939:626).

Some contact, sometimes resulting in intermarriage, soon occurred usually between Irish girls and second-generation Genoese men. But such contact did not greatly improve Irish-Italian relations, for, although it produced kinship among the few, it also caused yet another form of competition among Italian and Irish men.

After 1880, the conflict assumed a new character. As the southern Italians started pouring in, they became a more obvious target for the Irish than the Genoese had been. However, given their large numbers and their rather unrestrained methods of fighting, they soon became the lords of the streets. For the South Italians, it was "either a serious fight or no fight at all." And when it was a serious fight, any weapon was permissible, including the knife and the gun. The Irish, who had been accustomed to fighting only with fists, feet, knees, and blunt instruments, were naturally shocked. Whyte points out that, according to the unanimous testimony of all the Italians who spoke to him on this subject, "the introduction of the knife brought about a cessation of active hostilities" (Whyte, 1939:629). The younger generations, who found it easier to agree on the technology involved, continued to fight, but in a much milder form.

According to Whyte, the boundaries of the ethnic groups were sharply maintained throughout the Italian occupation.

However, this contention must be understood in context. As more Italians moved in, the physical frontier of their colony necessarily expanded. It follows that "the most bitter battles were fought along the advancing frontier of the Italian settlement, where sovereignty was still undecided." According to poll tax lists for available years, no large section of the North End had a fairly even mixture of Italians and Irish. In any given section, the people were usually either all Irish or all Italian, or else there was an 85 to 90 percent majority of one group (Whyte, 1939:630).

By 1910 to 1915, as the Italians became a majority, the purely interethnic struggle ended. A given street corner was the likely spot for a fight only as long as the Irish were residents of nearby areas. As they moved away, some could, and did, return to the familiar hang-outs at night. But under these conditions, it became too difficult to stay organized.

Conflict in the area did not cease altogether. The congestion of the ghetto, the persisting cultural diversities, and the sheer habit of fighting saw to that. A new phase was ushered in, which "might be called the Americanization of the conflict" (Whyte, 1939:632). Italians joined Irish gangs and Irish joined Italian gangs. Ethnic dislikes in the North End had not entirely vanished by 1915, but the actual hostilities, now carried on almost exclusively by young boys, had been largely transformed from Italian-Irish fights to inter-street fights. Any remaining interethnic clashes occurred only along sectional lines. "There is a long tradition of fighting between the Italian North End and the Irish Charlestown" (Whyte, 1939:634). By 1939 relations between the two North End groups were relatively peaceful. Whyte found that the type of antagonism most actively preserved was in the area of politics. In this, the history of the clash between the two groups reached its natural apogee.

The Italian-Irish conflict had begun as a competition for jobs and space with the contestants embittered by distinct cultural differences. Once the most basic needs of the Italians were satisfied, however, their attention was directed to the desirability of controlling, or at least sharing, the political machine in order to preserve their achievements and improve their position. Whyte noted that the Italians had to fight the Irish political machine and also overcome their own lack of unity. Still in 1939 there was a widespread feeling in the North End that Italians seeking political favors were discriminated against by the Irish and that nearly all the "good jobs," such as non-relief positions on the Works Progress Administration (WPA), were in the hands of the Irish (Whyte, 1939:640).

POLITICS. That was in 1939. Since then, matters have substantially changed. Throughout the city of Boston and in the state of Massachusetts, as indeed in other states, Italian Americans have taken an active part in politics. Since the late 1950s, for example, Massachusetts has had at least two state governors of Italian extraction.

No effort will be made here to compare the political participation and power of the Italian Americans relative to their numbers or to the Irish and other ethnic groups. It can be said with little risk of error that the Italians have been relatively slow and half-hearted participants in the political arena. Some possible reasons for this fact have already been mentioned. Italian immigrants arrived divided along regional, provincial, and to a lesser extent even municipal lines. The whims of their terrain and history were such that at the time of their arrival they had not developed a feeling of national unity and a consciousness of kind. As late as World War II, the great Italian novelist Carlo Levi could write from his place of exile among the peasants of southern Italy that these people had no national capital. However, if the idea of a capital could be stretched, New York deserved the title more than Rome or even Naples.

Novelists are privileged to dramatize a point. They rarely, however, shave facts of all their reality. More than among any other European people, the experience of the South Italian had included no participation in government. Matters political had been done for him—or more precisely *to* him. He had not possessed the franchise and other related political and civil rights. Whatever little contact he had had with government was hardly of the sort that left pleasant memories. His national government neglected him except when it assessed his heavy taxes. The bureaucrats humiliated, browbeat, and swindled him. As he saw it, he was consistently fleeced, robbed, and intimidated by all government officials. *Governo ladro* (thief of a government) is still an everyday imprecation throughout Italy.

Where there are political problems to be solved, political errors are invariably made. Where there are diverse political interests, there are sure to be political privileges and injustices. Where the political process is burdened with proliferating problems and an excessive fluidity of political interests, errors and privileges are bound to multiply. The image of politicians as "crooks" imported from the old country was often reinforced among Italian Americans by their political experiences in the new (Gans, 1962:169). Combine all these factors. Add to them the often-repeated consideration that Italian immigrants were poor and had little education, and, consequently, had relatively few men of wealth and education to lead them in the New World. The conclusion is inevitable that, as Glazer and Moynihan (1963:209) put it in the case of New York City, "the Italian Americans were slow and late in gaining an important place in the considerations of party leaders."

The Italian Americans still do not seem to have reached the point of maximizing their political potential. But their present status in the political affairs of the nation in general, and of the various states and cities where they are concentrated in particular, indicates that their early handicap is now being overcome. In New York City, for example, Italian Americans share equally with the Jews and the Irish in the political life of the great metropolis. They have had their mayors, their deputy mayors, their presidents of the City Council, and their Tammany Hall leaders, as well as other choice political positions. Indeed, in New York state, as in Massachusetts and Rhode Island, Italians have come near to establishing a political hegemony (Glazer and Moynihan, 1963: 215).

Various conditions have made this effective penetration of political systems inevitable. By 1930, a vast number of Italian immigrants had decided to settle permanently in America and had received their citizenship papers. At the same time, their American-born children represented a large proportion of the Italian American population. Many had received enough education to aim for something better than the lowly jobs of their parents. They quickly adopted three objectives that almost invariably lead to political activity: 1) jobs in the public administration; 2) avenues of economic and social improvement; and 3) protection for their businesses. Caroline Ware (1935:281) pointed out in 1935 that the creation of an increasing number of city jobs in Greenwich Village and the example of their Irish neighbors who held positions in City Hall proved a strong political stimulus to the Italians. In general, their desire to improve their social status grew as their numbers grew, and "politics was one of the few areas in which numbers rather than wealth or prestige counted."

The Italians, moreover, were among the first to take advantage of the business opportunities afforded by the illicit liquor industry of the Prohibition era. Activity in this area made political protection an immediate necessity, with the result that those interested either entered politics themselves or prodded trustworthy members of their group to do so. Political activity proved most attractive as an effective road to wealth, power, and prestige. In 1938, a federal report on the Italians of New York could already state that they were "one of the most active and politically conscious groups among New York's citizenry" (W.F.W.P.W.P.A., 1938:97).

The decade of the 1930s seems to have been critical for the Italian Americans' penetration of their political institutions and their coming of age as a major political force. The political story of one of their number, Fiorello H. La Guardia of New York, best exemplified their political maturation. According to his biographer Arthur Mann,

> Through La Guardia one can follow the struggle for power among the various immigrant groups; a Republican, he emerged as the first Italo-American successfully to challenge the political reign of Irish-Americans. His precedent has since become a trend of considerable sig-

nificance not only in his own metropolis, but in other cities of his state and in New England and elsewhere (Mann, 1959:11–12).

Born in Greenwich Village on December 11, 1882, La Guardia was the son of a Jewish-Italian mother and an Italian father. In 1885 his father joined the U. S. Army as chief musician, and for several years the family moved often, until they settled finally in Prescott, Arizona in 1892. In 1900 Fiorello entered the American consular service and went on duty in Budapest. Working his way up, he took over the one-man agency in Fiume until he quit in 1906 to return to the United States. In New York City, he worked for the immigration service while going to law school. Admitted to the bar in 1910, Fiorello began a private practice, with his principal clients working class people and immigrants. Soon thereafter he joined the Republican Club in his district. In 1916, he was elected representative to Congress from his Harlem district, and in 1919 he became a member of New York's Board of Aldermen. Unsuccessful as a candidate for mayor in 1921, La Guardia returned to Congress as representative in 1922, and he remained a representative until 1932. During these years he leaned politically to the left, breaking from the main fold of the Republicans and earning the reputation of a liberal, a progressive, and at times a socialist (Mann, 1965:25–36).

In 1934 La Guardia became mayor of New York, and during his term in office compiled one of the most colorful and inspiring legacies in the history of that city. Almost defensively proud of his Italian ancestry, he received throughout his political career constant and hearty support from his Italian constituency. But Fiorello, the Little Flower, was a unique individual. He represented the Italian Americans' coming of age not only as a political group but also as a people who were American enough to have substantial political appeal well beyond their own tribe.

> To put it sociologically, La Guardia was a marginal man who lived on the edge of many cultures, so that he was able to face in several directions at the same time. . . . this unorthodox Republican . . . spoke, according to the

occasion, in Yiddish, Hungarian, German, Italian, Ser-
bian-Croatian, or plain New York English. . . . Born in
Greenwich Village yet raised in Arizona, married first to a
Catholic and then to a Lutheran but himself a Mason and
an Episcopalian, Fiorello La Guardia was a Mr. Brother-
hood Week all by himself. . . . He was so many persons
in one, so uniquely unparochial in that most parochial of
cities, that New Yorkers of nearly every sort were able to
identify themselves with him, although rarely for the
same reasons. The hyphens of this many-hyphenated
American were like magnets (Mann, 1959:21).

La Guardia's initial ventures into political activity, however,
were based on his support in the New York Italian colony. In
promoting himself with the leaders of his ethnic group, he was
proceeding in the manner of his Irish counterparts in Tammany Hall, who rose to political power with the help of the
Irish. Mann (1959:143) has this to say about La Guardia's
return to politics after his unsuccessful first attempt to become
mayor of New York in 1921:

If La Guardia had no Eleanor Roosevelt, Louis Howe, Al
Smith, or an already existing and friendly organization
to help his comeback, he could count on the support of
his loyal Italian followers. As *Il Vaglio*, an Italian-lan-
guage newspaper saw it, the political leader La Guardia
gave the lie to bigots who held that Italo-Americans were
fit only for ditchdigging and organ-grinding.

Italian Americans and American Society

The theme of this book is the adaptation of Italian Americans
to American culture and their gradual absorption into American society. Conceptually, we are concerned with *acculturation*
and *assimilation,* two terms often used interchangeably to convey a variety of meanings.

The best known definition of "acculturation" was provided
by a Subcommittee on Acculturation, a group appointed in the
middle 1930s by the Social Science Research Council specific-

ally to clarify this important dimension of cultural change. The definition produced by the subcommittee stated that acculturation "comprehends those phenomena which result when groups of individuals having different cultures come into continuous first-hand contact, with subsequent changes in the original cultural patterns of either or both groups" (Redfield *et al.*, 1936:149).

For general purposes, this brief definition is probably the best available because it takes into account the obviously important two-way effect of cultural contact. However, we are more concerned with the modification of Italian culture in contact with American culture than with the changes in American culture that resulted from the Italian influence. Hence, one of the several definitions of acculturation given by Robert Park and Ernest Burgess (1921:735) is more directly to our point. They, like most other sociologists, preferred the term assimilation.

> Assimilation is a process of interpenetration and fusion in which persons and groups acquire the memories, sentiments, and attitudes of other persons or groups, and, by sharing their experience and history, are incorporated with them in a common cultural life.

A few years later, Park produced a specification that is particularly useful for our purposes although he focused exclusively on the immigrant, while we are discussing both immigrant and his descendants. Park (1930:281) stated:

> In the United States an immigrant is ordinarily considered assimilated as soon as he has acquired the language and the social ritual of the native community and can participate, without encountering prejudice, in the common life, economic and political. The common sense view of the matter is that an immigrant is assimilated as soon as he has shown that he can "get on in the country." This implies among other things that in all the ordinary affairs of life he is able to find a place in the community on the basis of his individual merits without invidious or qualifying reference to his racial origin or to his cultural inheritance.

I have suggested that various characteristics of the Italian immigrants very likely impeded their assimilation in American society. Among these were the Italians' previous poverty and illiteracy; their apolitical tradition; their original intention to make their fortune quickly and then return to the old society; their arrival in rapid succession and in very great numbers, a fact that facilitated endeavors to recreate old world conditions; their arrival at a time when further immigration was looked upon as inimical to American culture and interests; and several other factors concerning religion, language, labor contracts, and the like.

THE PROMISED LAND. There is still another factor that played a very considerable part in hindering the Italian's Americanization. This is the image of America he had formulated before he came to this country, as well as what happened to that image after he arrived on these shores. The Italians tended to idealize America before they came. To them, it was "the promised land"—a heaven in more senses than one. In America, so the story went, a man could progress just because he was a man, not merely because he was the son of so-and-so. This conception was fostered by labor agents, by hungry dreamers, and by returned immigrants who found it less damaging to their ego to speak of their successes than of their failures. In America one could freely strain his talents, skills, and ambitions to the limit in the search for wealth and the good life, and his struggle would be met with approbation. Here if the streets were not exactly paved with gold, at least the poor, if diligent, could expect to gain it from the fat payrolls of businessmen hungry for laborers. Here a man could look at his neighbor straight in the eye and say: "I am a man, and by the grace of my labor, a respectable one at that."

The facts, of course, were different. For most, at least initially, America was a big disappointment—with respect to the noble ideas, if not entirely to the basics of economics. The America they found was a society of angry men ready to violate not only the immigrants' conception of the promised land, but even their conception of themselves as honorable men as well as whatever sense of peoplehood and nationality they might have had. The immigrants were not viewed merely as dirty, greasy, stinking, and dangerous. They were also dirty, greasy, stinking, and dangerous "wops" and "Eyetalians." This turned out to be a world where, by sweating blood twelve hours a day and six days a week, one could indeed earn enough money to clothe himself comfortably, fill his stomach with spaghetti and beans, and even save a few dollars a week toward that coveted plot of land in Italy. But it was also a world in which the sacred motto seemed to be, in an anticipated variation of Orwell's classic dictum, "Every man has the right to survive provided that he does not let himself be overwhelmed by another."

The indignant Irish, the superior and alarmed "Americans," the avaricious and scheming *padroni,* the uncertain employment, the inevitable job accidents, the long hours spent bending over pick and shovel listening to the snarling voice of the boss, the ethnic jokes and curses, the putrid air of the ghetto cells, the sick children, the children returning home from school wishing to know why it was bad to be a "guinea," the beatings by the police and the roving gangs, the thefts, the debts—"Oh God," an old immigrant said to me some time ago, "you have no idea how many times I yearned for an armful of straw on anybody's farm in the old country. But I couldn't go back. I first had to pay my debts, and then maybe save a little something in order not to return home empty-handed. . . . By then America actually wasn't so bad. Either she had changed, or I had changed. Anyway, I never went back to Italy." (It was amazing how the suffering in America made attractive even the inferno of the old life!)

Robert Park and Herbert Miller (1921:46–47) quote another immigrant as follows:

All the time I hear about the grand city of New York. They say it is something to surprise everyone. I learn New York is twice, three, four, ten times bigger than Italian city. Maybe it is better than Milano. Maybe it is better than Naples.

"The land of the free and the home of the brave"—I am young and I think that is beautiful land. I hear such fine words like "liberty," "democracy," "equality," "fra-

ternity," and I like this high principles. The people say it
is the country where you are your own boss, where you
may receive money on your word, where there is trust
and confidence, so that America look like a blessed country, and I think I am going to great city, to grand
country, to better world, and my heart develop big
admiration and a great, noble sentiment for America
and the Americano.

I arrive in New York. You think I find here my idea? . . .

Here and there, an Italian immigrant poured out his disappointment and his resentment in a novel or an autobiography.
Several were influenced by sociological thought. One of them,
Constantine Panunzio (1921:184–185), revealed in vivid terms
the vicissitudes of his own drama of life in the New World. Of
particular interest is his discussion of the changes that occurred in him as a result of his first experiences here. One
concerned his conception of America. "The first of these
[changes] was the loss of that trustful simplicity which I
brought to America with me. Then the persons I met were
my friends. I believed in them, I believed their words, I
trusted them." Exploitation and suffering changed that. "I
gradually came to believe that I was surrounded by enemies,
and that my own attitude must always be one of self-defense."
Another vivid description of the Italian American immigrants' experience (also one of the classics of American labor
literature) is Pietro Di Donato's *Christ in Concrete*. The book
draws a pathetic picture of Italians living in squalor, the endless hazards of an uncertain job, children orphaned and helpless, the injustices of a foreign and hostile bureaucracy.

Husband of Annunziata, Geremio is the foreman of a construction crew. On a cold day the unfinished structure of a
building collapses because of faulty underpinning, and Geremio and others are killed. At twelve, Paul is the oldest of
Annunziata's children, and he desperately attempts to learn
bricklaying, his father's old profession, in order to provide
food for his mother and his seven brothers and sisters. Although he has difficulty at first because of his slight size, he
nevertheless almost magically possesses his father's skill. A
few years go by, and at sixteen Paul moves on to work on the

big skyscrapers downtown. But personal tragedy follows him, and he witnesses the violent death of his godfather, and a while later the quiet death of his mother. No longer a boy, Paul becomes mother and father to his brothers and sisters (Di Donato, 1937).

More poignant still is Di Donato's account of Annunziata's and Paul's reflections on the events of the day they sought compensation for Geremio's death. After an unsuccessful visit to the Workmen's Compensation Bureau where Mr. Murdin, Geremio's boss, made it appear that Geremio and the other Italians were responsible for the collapse when it was actually Murdin's fault, Annunziata and Paul that night think of the day's events. Their reflections suggest the nature of the immigrant's experience with American government and officials. Di Donato (1937:176–178) writes:

Back again in the sanctity of night's cave Annunziata and Paul lay communing with the poor's Christ. As they spoke to him the ghostly army of maimed shabby humans with the seeking faces filed humbly past them in the corridors of the vast prison where there were numerous chambers, and signs sticking out over the doors that said: "Clinic" — "Disability" — "Men's Toilet" — "Adjustments"—"Death Claims." And they saw the sleek flaccid state employees, and heard the correct American voices of Parker, Murdin, Norr, Kagan and other passionless soaped tongues that conquered with grammatic clean-cut: "What is your name? Your maiden name? How many children? Where were you born? This way please. Sit here please. Please answer yes or no. Eyetalians insist on hurting themselves when not personally supervised . . . directly his fault . . . substantiate . . . disclaim . . . liability . . . case adjourned." And they saw the winning smiles that made them feel they had conspired with Geremio to kill himself so that they could present themselves there as objects of pity and then receive American dollars for nothing. The smiles that made them feel they had undressed in front of these gentlemen and revealed dirty underwear. The smiles that smelled of refreshing toothpaste and considered flesh. The smiles that made them feel they were un-Godly and greasy pagan Christians; the smiles that told them they did not belong in the Workmen's Compensation Bureau.

Where did these men come from? Who are they? Where and how do they live? For whom do they weep, and to whom do they pray? . . .

And Paul clutched his pillow.

O God above, what world and country are we in? We didn't mean to be wrong.

One may wonder why, after their vision of the promised land was shattered, so many Italians settled permanently in America. The reasons are many and complex. Although most immigrants were single men who planned to return home as soon as possible, some came as family units, fully intending to stay. These few had made a clean break with the old community, and it was both humiliating and prohibitively expensive to admit failure and return. Second, despite a certain craving for the old life, in moments of extreme stress, all immigrants—whether as single men or as members of family units—usually remembered what had been equally unbearable and economically much less rewarding than life in the New World. Third, given the debts to be paid and the low wages received, many immigrants found themselves drudging away for many years in order not to go back home empty-handed. In the meantime America changed for the better, opportunities multiplied, the immigrants became adjusted and accustomed to the new life. The thought, moreover, came to mind to those who had left their families in Italy that everything would be easier if they had their families with them to provide them with the comforts of love and a home life. Many married men, therefore, sent for their dear ones, while the bachelors either found a wife in America among the daughters of older immigrants or went back home for an "honest girl" who would give them emotional support in the new society.

CRIME. The Italian immigrants and their children found themselves in a situation in which their person and ethnicity were degraded, their manners and habits were disdained, their work was to a considerable extent exploited, their domicile was unhealthy, their rights were all too often trampled upon. Demoralization thrived in such conditions. Sometimes it produced reactions that go under the name of criminal behavior.

This reaction to a degraded environment was especially prevalent among the second generation. The old-timer still had a star in the East feebly shining for him, to which he sometimes longingly turned for comfort. Moreover, by the very fact of his immigration, he was a special sort of man. He had a special mission to lift his family from misery and squalor. The ardor with which he pursued this goal tended to mitigate his demoralization. But his son, that marginal man *par excellence*, was in serious trouble.

In the discussion of intergenerational conflict we noted how easy it was for the immigrant's children to become estranged from their parents' culture and how they often escaped the restraining influence of familial authority. The "old greasers" were often viewed as obstacles to acceptance and respectability. The second generation found itself living in two different social worlds. For instance, the middle class teacher at school and papa at home defined the same situation in very different ways. The second-generation child, especially the boy who was never insulated from the nasty world by the sanctuary of the home, could hardly conform to one moral code without being delinquent with respect to the other. A combination of moral confusion and ethnic self-hatred frequently resulted in legally "delinquent" behavior. A perceptive observer of immigrant society, Harvey Zorbaugh (1929:177) pointed out in 1929:

> Out of this situation . . . arises the gang, affording the boy a social world in which he finds his only status and recognition. But it is by conforming to delinquent patterns that he achieves status in the gang. And every boy in Little Hell is a member of a gang. This is substantially the process of disorganization of the Sicilian boy of the second generation. Out of it grows all manner of social disorganization.

Twenty-six years later, this engaging idea was elaborated in one of the most interesting discussions of the American youth gang. Examining the organized behavior of delinquent boys, Albert Cohen (1955:121) argued that the "delinquent subculture" is a way of dealing with the working class boys' problems of adjustment to a middle class society.

> These problems are chiefly status problems: certain children are denied status in the respectable society because they cannot meet the criteria of the respectable status system. The delinquent subculture deals with these problems by providing criteria of status which these children *can* meet.

It is probably neither common nor healthy for men to endlessly crave admission into groups that are persistently closed to them. The deeply ingrained need for social approbation and the need for self-respect are too closely tied together, to allow a man to continue a pursuit that yields continuous self-degradation. Chances are that, after trying and failing for a time, the individual will turn to a group that readily grants him social approval and a healthy self-image. The basic meaning in the tale of the fox and the sour grapes reaches the heart of a human universal.

In the delinquent boy's case, the delinquent culture is a substitute, with a vengeance, for what is denied to him by the "respectable" society. As Cohen states (1955:129), "The hallmark of the delinquent subculture is the explicit and wholesale repudiation of middle-class standards and the adoption of their very antithesis." The delinquent subculture is *"nonutilitarian, malicious* and *negativistic."* Do respectable people value property highly? Then why not attack it by stealing? Not for profit, however, for that would implicitly honor one of the cardinal virtues of the decent society, but just "for the hell of it." Do respectable people diligently and studiously elaborate plans for the future, emphasizing long-run goals? Then the delinquent boys practice a short-run hedonism. "They are impatient, impetuous and out for 'fun,' with little heed to the remoter gains and costs." Do nice people tend toward diffuse relations and sentiments? Then, "relations with gang members tend to be intensely solidary and imperious. Relations with other groups tend to be indifferent, hostile or rebellious" (Cohen, 1955:25–31).

The delinquent gang thus affords the rejected and resentful

working class boy a chance to strike at those values and norms of the respectable society that views him as a social outcast. Even more important, in so doing, the gang not only makes overt aggression possible but also legitimates it (Cohen, 1955: 131) and awards social status in direct proportion to the hostility displayed toward the "respectable" society.

There is no clear-cut evidence that the gang is a school for socialization in the world of crime. But the biographies of many criminals suggest precisely this type of association. Data on crime rates by ethnicity are extremely scarce and almost impossible to obtain. The little that is available, however, indicates that, in general (Cressey, 1966:153–155; see also Nelli, 1969:384), foreign-born Italian Americans have *lower* crime rates than native whites. The second generation, however, has almost double the rate of the first generation. According to the data given by the Workers of the Federal Writers' Project, Works Progress Administration (Wickersham Report) on all foreign-born individuals arrested or arraigned in New York magistrates' courts as of 1930, Italians contributed 542 cases per 10,000 of their population. This figure was higher by about 100 cases than the ratio for all foreign-born groups, but it compared favorably with the ratio for all native Americans (616), with that of certain other immigrant groups (for example, Greeks: 3,152), and with the ratio for the city as a whole (559). On the other hand, in 1929 the crime rate of the second generation exceeded that of the Italian-born by 75 percent (W.F.W.P.W.P.A., 1938:54–56).

Some of the possible sociological causes of crime among Italian Americans are probably specific to them, while others are general to all immigrant groups, indeed perhaps to all underprivileged people. Previously, I have emphasized the sense of self-degradation that developed among children of people whose culture was looked upon with scorn by American society. Out of the humiliation and resentment generated by this situation sometimes came mischief that clashed with the legal institutions of the larger society.

Other factors include the well-documented opportunities for crime offered by Prohibition; the abject conditions of the slums, which naturally produced behavior punishable in the eyes of middle class society; and what might be termed the *curse of the doubt* that among the poor parallels the proverbial "benefit of the doubt" enjoyed by the middle class. Criminologists have frequently noted that the lower classes, the poor, and the unwanted in general are taken in by the police for acts that are either disregarded when committed by members of the upper classes or considered temporary aberrations. A poor boy commits a crime because he is "plainly criminal"; a rich boy merely does "a fool thing" because he is "sowing wild oats." This naturally inflates the crime rate of the poor. When the underprivileged Italians and their children found themselves in the inimitable slums of the American city, they had this factor going against them.

Two additional factors productive of criminal behavior deserve special attention. One concerns the Italians' experience with crime before they came to these shores; the other relates to a peculiar ethos in American culture in which the emphasis on success is so great that it encourages achievement at all costs.

America has a long tradition as a refuge for criminals, among the many other kinds of people it has received. It is quite possible that, with the exception of England, Italy has sent over more than her share of thugs. A number of Italians had been embroiled in the affairs and activities of certain groups of criminals known collectively as the *mafia*. No one knows precisely how the *mafia* came to be, exactly how it operates, or how it is organized. The failure of countless efforts to reliably answer such questions may reflect the fact that historical and social researchers are a bit too much concerned with fixing the specific point in time for various phenomena and assigning them specific forms of organization (usually of the rational-bureaucratic type). What one might term the "natural-cavern" image of phenomena—the view of things as having their creation deeply rooted in time and surrounding conditions—has few or no practitioners in our midst. Little wonder, for such a view would require countless and extremely minute measurements that invariably are arduous and often impossible. The end result of the rationalistic approach is a series of neat little schemes that impose the most improbable straight jackets on reality, while clouding the vision of him who seeks it. Broad, sweeping strokes of the brush may be awkward, but they are often more revealing.

The *mafia,* or some variation thereof, while reaching its highest expression on the island of Sicily, probably first occurred as a recognizable phenomenon toward the end of the eighteenth century throughout southern Italy. Perhaps the best way to acquire "a feel" for it (for that is all we can hope for) is to imagine it developing as a force of reaction against the intensified abuses of a moribund feudalism. To be sure, any historian can point to instances in which the *mafia* was an instrument, not against, but in the hands of, the feudal nobility. But that merely reveals something about the mutability of human phenomena and the corruptibility of human ideals.

The *mafia* probably had its roots in the absolute necessity of the southern Italian masses to defend their families, their honor, their source of livelihood, and their very life at a time when those who possessed secular and ecclesiastical authority were renouncing all obligations of law and order (Hobsbawn, 1959:32) to the people while at the same time robbing them of whatever land they possessed, molesting their wives and daughters, imposing intolerable taxation, and inflicting all manner of moral as well as corporal punishments. Originally, the *mafia* consisted of little more than scattered little groups of peasants, often outlaws, who found in each other's strength and resolve the basis of a new moral and social order.

Even today, throughout the agricultural regions of southern Italy, one finds in many a village a *sacra famiglia* (sacred family), an organization of local young men whose express purpose is to defend the "honor and property" of the community in general and of their own families in particular. The organization, sometimes termed *Umiltà* (Humility), has elaborate hierarchies of offices and functions, colorful ceremonies and rituals, and a language in which terms like "honor," "blood," "family," "man," and "wisdom" have a very special significance. So noble are the official intentions of the *sacra famiglia,* and so religious the members' conception of its function within the local scheme of things, that when a new member is installed in the organization, after a full six months of being *in bello* (under scrutiny), the chief tells him, "From this moment on, you are not a mere member of the mob [the populace] but a man healthy, wise, and holy."

The ontogeny of a local *Umiltà* discloses a great deal about the phylogeny of the *mafia*. It unmistakably reveals how a corrupt individual can rise to the top of the power hierarchy and, aided by a small group of lieutenants, use the organization to commit under the protection of secrecy those very wrongs that it was supposedly established to prevent. Thefts, acts of terrorism against the weak, and abuses against helpless women are the specialty of the *mafiosi*. Sometimes, after a period of control, the leader becomes isolated by his own abuses and leaves the scene—usually either because he lands in jail or because he is slain. His followers disband, and a group of young men, eager for fun, new experience, power, and the highest kind of honor that can befall a peasant among his peers in the village, again organize the *Umiltà* in pursuit of noble ideals.

Little is known about interorganizational connections between communities, although there is little doubt that some ties exist. As a rough generalization, it may be stated that the degree of interorganizational contact is in direct proportion to the volume and economic significance of the local organizations' activities. When, as in the Palermo area in Sicily, a number of local *mafia*-like organizations flourish and seek to extend their area of activity and influence, interorganizational clashes are likely to develop. These conflicts are never fully eliminated, but the clashes invariably generate attempts at reconciliation. And from this flows the sort of phenomenon known as *mafia*. It thrives in situations of corruption and relative normlessness. It could not be avoided in the New World.

Some basic techniques of organization of the American *mafia* came from Sicily. The *mafia*'s success and growth, however, were unquestionably fostered by conditions arising from the monumental political error that was Prohibition (see Nelli, 1969:385), by the betrayal experienced when high ideals of democracy were rendered a sham by egoism and hypocrisy, by the festering sore that was the *padrone* system, by the corruptibility of self-seeking officials—both private and public—and by the pathetic fears and helplessness of the early immigrants.

Whatever the causes, the *mafia* has done great damage to the Italians in America as well as to the larger society. Before directing its attention to broader horizons, it exploited the weak and defenseless immigrants, striking terror in their hearts and undermining their respect for American laws and customs. In 1921 Park and Miller (1921:241) argued that "the spirit of *mafia, camorra,* and vendetta, the most notorious of the Italian heritages, which developed here into the Black Hand activities, has had a paralyzing effect on the development of Italian life."

Today the *mafia* has no more hold on the many millions of Italian Americans than does Chinese communism or Italian soccer. Yet, the growth of the *mafia,* (otherwise known as "syndicate," "mob," or "*cosa nostra*") into national prominence under the aegis of crooked politicians, frightened or grasping businessmen, and corrupt police officers sometimes makes "big crime" sound peculiarly Italian. According to two recent articles in *Life* magazine (Smith, 1967), there are about 5,000 members of *cosa nostra,* all of whom are of Italian extraction, mostly Sicilian. *Cosa nostra* is a cartel of twenty-four semi-independent "families" that vary widely in size (from 20 to 1,000 members) and in their importance in the rackets. Each family has its own internal hierarchy headed by a boss (see also Anderson, 1965).

The *mafia's* success depends on an operation called the "fix," a working arrangement with key police, elected officials, and business and union executives. Most of the time it involves a simple money pay-off from the mob in return for favors received. Since the "bought" person must be in a position of power or authority in order to deliver his favors, "the cardinal principle of the fix is immutable—i.e., be with winners. Politically, this is conducive to bipartisanship." Examples of fixes range from one-million-dollar bribes to small pay-offs to officials for such favors as "the passing along of information that comes over their desks" and warning the organization of possible official action against it.

The mob makes its profits in two principal ways—through illegal betting on sports events, "a business thoroughly dominated by the Mob," and by means of *legitimate* business investment. The *mafia* thrives by exploiting the urge to gamble. Each year, presumably it handles $20 billion in illegal bets, of which it keeps $7 billion profit. The mob's involvement, of course, goes further than just taking bets. Often it attempts to use athletes or coaches either to gain information or to buy them off to affect the outcome of a game.

Interestingly enough, operating through and acquiring legitimate businesses is attracting increasing attention among the *mafiosi* in their search for profits. This trend represents a distinct move on the part of these twentieth-century "robber barons" toward legitimacy. The development suggests that since the big *mafia* chiefs are of Italian extraction, fifty years or so hence there are likely to be a great many peers of the Rockefellers, Morgans, Mellons, and the like having names that end in a vowel or claiming ancestors among those who had such names.

No disrespect is meant for the "big families" of today. But money, like wine, does have a way of growing old and sublime. It is even possible that rarely if ever can great wealth be achieved without intrigue and scandal, without twisting the spirit and the arm of the law. The biographies and autobiographies of those who are suggestively called "robber barons," together with reports about their business deals, will reveal to the curious citizen the extent to which they took, by hook or by crook, from the little man, the petty businessman, the government, and the soldier dying at the front for liberty, democracy, and "free enterprise." There are many ways of breaking the law. Much of the history of America's "big families" is a history of "war-profits conspiracies," airplane scandals, charges of defrauding government on war contracts, attorney generals acting as "fixers" for the wealthy, the Teapot Dome scandal, the Shipping Board scandal, price-fixing scandals, oil and land "grabs," airmail contracts collusively obtained, and so forth in an endless list of "free enterprise" deals (Lundberg, 1937:especially chap. 6).

Or consider the history of the big landed estates that developed along the American frontier. An idea of the grabbing, the intrigues, and the law of might that prevailed is given by Hollywood's recurrent theme of the land-grabbing scoundrel. In the movies the thief and his hired straw-chewing, black-jacketed gunslinger always lose out in the end to the law-abiding, courageous, redeeming hero. But, of course, this falls a bit short of the historical truth.

It is possible that the desire for power and wealth is nowhere and at no time innocent of the will to use all means necessary for their achievement. And this takes us to the second factor, previously referred to, which to some indeterminate extent has been conducive to deviant behavior among Italian Americans and other minority groups.

In what is probably the best known essay in sociology, Robert Merton (1957:134) has advanced the hypothesis that "aberrant behavior may be regarded sociologically as a symptom of dissociation between culturally prescribed aspirations and socially structured avenues for realizing these aspirations." Merton has found that contemporary American culture approximates a type in which great emphasis is placed upon certain goals of success without the equivalent emphasis on the institutional means necessary for such success. For instance, the goal of attaining monetary rewards is so entrenched in American culture that, "Americans are bombarded on every side by precepts which affirm the right or, often, the duty of retaining the goal even in the face of repeated frustration" (Merton, 1957:137).

Given a disjunction between goals and means for achieving the goals, what are some of the possible modes of adaptation among the American people? Merton singles out five major ones: conformity, ritualism, retreatism, rebellion, and *innovation*. The innovative reaction is particularly pertinent to the point under discussion. Innovation is a response which, on the one hand, is structurally encouraged by the disjunction between the goals of success and the means for their achievement. On the other hand, criminal innovation is condoned by a tendency among American people to tolerate, indeed admire and esteem, successful scoundrels and knaves. To Merton (1957:146) "Al Capone represents the triumph of amoral intelligence over morally prescribed 'failure,' when the channels of vertical mobility are closed or narrowed *in a society which places a high premium on economic affluence and social ascent for* all *its members.*"

In a similar vein, William Foote Whyte (1943:273–274) wrote of Boston in 1943:

> Our society places a high value upon social mobility. According to tradition, the working-man starts in at the bottom and by means of intelligence and hard work climbs the ladder of success. It is difficult for the Cornerville man to get onto the ladder, even on the bottom rung. His district has become popularly known as a disordered and lawless community. He is an Italian, and the Italians are looked upon by upper-class people as among the least desirable of the immigrant peoples. . . . Even if the man can get a grip on the bottom rung, he finds the same factors prejudicing his advancement. Consequently, one does not find Italian names among the leading officers of the old established business of Eastern City. The Italians have had to build up their own business hierarchies, and, when the prosperity of the twenties came to an end, it became increasingly difficult for the newcomer to advance in this way. . . . At the same time the society holds out attractive rewards in terms of money and material possessions to the "successful" man. For most Cornerville people these rewards are available only through advancement in the world of rackets and politics.

In short, deviant behavior among minority groups often occurs because, ironically, they take to heart the lofty promises of the American Dream although they are not allowed the legitimate means with which to realize it. A sobering thought will almost unavoidably occur to the sociologist who is keen to the ideas of "system" and "equilibrium" in scientific research. Crime and rackets help produce the degree of equilibrium and stability of relations among social classes to which the American Dream makes reference. To put it bluntly, these "pathological" occurrences help make the American Dream real by opening avenues of success for the socially underprivileged. In the process, being phenomena naturally attracted to the loci of power, crime and rackets become deeply and intricately entangled in our political process.

Daniel Bell's (1960:115–136) excellent analysis of the relation between crime and politics in American life points out that each ethnic group intent upon achieving wealth and recognition in America—trying to "get on in the country," as Park put it earlier—has produced prominent underworld figures. The politically powerful Irish gangsters gave way to Arnold Rothstein and his fellows in the 1920s, and the Jews, in turn, gave way to Frank Costello and his compatriots in the middle 1930s.

What is even more interesting is that the association between crime and politics is not due solely to the fact that both are power phenomena. Alas, it would almost seem that there is a need for crime in politics. How else can one explain the frequently documented cases of friendship between public officials and public swindlers? And how else can one explain the public, not to mention the private, honors that some public officials sometimes bestow upon gangsters? In a discussion of the spectacular funerals of Chicago gangsters in the 1920s, Landesco (1929:chap. 25) pointed out how the obligations of prominent citizens and politicians came to the surface on such occasions. Take, for instance, the splendorous funeral of James (Big Jim) Colosimo, a powerful chief of the underground who was killed in May 1920. His cortege included many prominent politicians. An alderman and a state senator were pallbearers. Standing by, as honorary pallbearers, were eight other aldermen, three judges, several individuals who later became judges, and two congressmen, one of whom later became speaker of the United States House of Representatives.

INTERMARRIAGE. While deviant behavior and political participation are good indicators of problems and degrees of acculturation in American society, data on intermarriage tell us something about social amalgamation and the disposition to lose ethnic identification. There are no data to indicate the rate of marriage by Italian Americans in general with other ethnic groups. However, a very interesting study of Italian Americans in New Haven, Connecticut for the period 1870–1950 throws considerable light on this question, although apparently it concerns largely the second generation.

Ruby Jo Reeves Kennedy (1952) found that the Italians, after the Jews, had consistently had the highest in-marriage rate of seven ethnic groups considered (Jewish, Italian, British-American, Irish, Polish, German, and Scandinavian). This fact, however, was partly due, in 1950 at least, to the fact that the Italians constituted about one-fourth of the New Haven population, a fact that must have made it particularly tempting for them to marry within their own group.

The rate of in-group marriage among Italians, as among other ethnic groups, decreased as time went by. Thus, while in 1900, the first year for which the data on Italians are shown, 97.7 percent of Italian marriages were strictly endogamous, the corresponding rate in 1950 was 76.7 percent. Furthermore, the Italians were the only large group except the Poles who showed an increasing tendency toward out-marriage between 1940 and 1950. Focusing on changes in the decade 1940–1950, Kennedy found that in 1950 the British-Americans married Irish and Italians with equal frequency, whereas in 1940 the Irish were preferred to the Italians. Again, in 1950 the Germans married as many Italians as Scandinavians. Italians expanded their out-marriage choices to include Scandinavians and Jews for the first time in 1950.

Such findings suggest that the rate of ethnic intermarriage has been increasing in the later generations, and will doubtless be still greater among generations to come. However, intermarriage will probably be hindered by religious differences even when ethnic differences are no longer relevant. Far from supporting the idea of a single melting pot, Kennedy's data (1952; cf. Hollingshead, 1950) suggested that intermarriage actually produced a triple-melting-pot type of assimilation, with "Catholicism, Protestantism, and Judaism serving as the three fundamental bulwarks." A large proportion of all intermarriages appeared to be homogeneous with respect to religious ties. Thus, in 1950, 70 percent of the British-American, German, and Scandinavian marriages were consummated among members of these three Protestant groups; nearly 73 percent of all Catholics (Italians, Irish, Poles) married among themselves; while almost all Jews (96 percent) married other Jews (Kennedy, 1952:59).

It is possible, however, that under the influence of increasing secularization and the culturally equalizing effects of mass communications, ethico-religious bonds will weaken to a much greater extent and allow a higher degree of freedom in the choice of marital partners and, hence, of personal relationships in the most intimate aspect of the human existence.

PREJUDICE. Studies of ethnic prejudice and related phenomena encourage the optimists to think along these lines. A study by Robin Williams and associates (1964) is especially worthy of note in this respect. The study, which spans a period of eight years (from 1948 to 1956) presents findings on majority-minority group relations for Elmira, New York; Steubenville, Ohio; Bakersfield, California; Savannah, Georgia; and (in lesser detail) for twenty other cities in the United States.

Consider the answers to the interview question, "As you see it, are Italians today demanding more than they have a right to or not?" Out of 451 cases in the majority group in Hometown (Elmira), 8 percent answered yes and 92 percent answered no to this question (Williams, 1964:51)—a remarkable change, one can be sure, from what would have been the case during the early years of the Italians' experience in Elmira. Again, findings concerning the "distasteful score," which "indicated the number of situations in which respondents said they would find contact with ethnic individuals distasteful to them," exhibited the following distribution of distastefulness with respect to Afro-Americans, Jews, and Italians on the part of the majority group in Hometown (Williams, 1964: 410–411):

	Score	Toward Afro-Americans	Toward Jews	Toward Italians
Low	0	1%	41%	56%
	1	13%	30%	23%
	2	12%	15%	10%
	3	26%	8%	5%
High	4	48%	6%	6%

This table indicates that most of the majority group displayed no distaste for contact with Italians and only a very small minority showed a high degree of aversion to such contact. Nevertheless, a certain amount of prejudice still remained, although less with respect to Jews and Italians than with the Black Americans. Consider, next, more specific questions of "distastefulness." To the question, "Do you think you would ever find it a little distasteful to eat at the same table with an Italian?", 7 percent out of a total of 494 cases in the majority group of Hometown answered yes. The corresponding figures were 9 and 91 percent, respectively, for the Jews and 50 percent yes, 50 percent no for the Afro-Americans. A question concerning whether the respondent would find it a little distasteful "to go to a party and find that most of the people are Italians," elicited yes answers from 24 percent of the people asked. The corresponding percentages for partying with Jews and Black Americans were 32 and 81, respectively (Williams, 1964:52).

The minorities themselves were not free of prejudice. For instance, we find that 48 percent of the Hometown Italians (slightly *less* than the 50 percent of the majority group) found it a little distasteful to eat at the same table with a Black American, and 84 percent (slightly *more* than the 81 percent of the majority group) found it distasteful to be at a party where most of the people were Black. The Italians displayed appreciably less prejudice against eating and going to parties with Jews than the majority group. Thus, while 9 percent of the majority group felt eating with Jews was distasteful and 32 percent felt partying with Jews was displeasing, the corresponding percentages among the Italians were only 5 and 13 (Williams, 1964:52).

The Italians' relative lack of prejudice with respect to the Jews may reflect the fact that there have been relatively few competitive encounters between the two groups in this country. Jews, for instance, never found it congenial to engage in unskilled occupations. Barring a few exceptions, they have not faced each other as antagonists in any of the important aspects of adaptation to American society. What is more, in the old society relations between the two groups were reasonably good. As Maurice Davie (1947:74) pointed out, the Jews in Italy, though a small minority, have a "long favored position." The real reasons for this situation are not clear. However, in view of the fact that religious understandings have often gotten in the way of kindly relations between Christians and Jews, it is worth noting that Italians have always understood that if the Jews "killed" the Christ, they also gave birth to him. In any case in his study of refugees Davie was not surprised to find that Italian Jewish refugees in America were more favorably disposed toward returning to the homeland than German, Austrian, Polish, Czech and Hungarian Jews.

In conclusion, although it is probably unrepresentative, the little evidence available suggests that prejudice against Italians in America has sunk a great deal from what it must have been fifty or sixty years ago. A small amount of direct evidence concerning the curve of prejudice against Italians in America is available. In 1932 Daniel Katz and Kenneth Braly (1933: 280–290) asked undergraduate students at Princeton to select from a list of eighty-four terms which five were most characteristic of certain nationalities, among them the Italians. Fifty-three percent of the respondents considered the Italians "artistic." Next most often mentioned were "impulsive," "passionate," "quick-tempered," "musical," and "imaginative," in that order.

Eighteen years later, in 1950, G. M. Gilbert (1951:245–254) repeated the experiment at the same university. He found that, although the old stereotypes tended to recur, they were a great deal weaker. Compare the results of the two studies concerning the six characteristics most often selected by Princeton students as typical of Italian Americans:

Characteristic	1932	1950
Artistic	53	28
Impulsive	44	19
Passionate	37	25
Quick-tempered	35	15
Musical	32	22
Imaginative	30	20

Based on his study, Gilbert (1951:249) made the following comment:

> The artistic and hot-tempered Italian, representing a cross between the temperamental maestro and the cheerful organ-grinder, is still with us; but . . . he is only a faded image of his former self. There is a considerable reduction in the artistic cluster—*artistic, musical, imaginative*—as well as the temperamental one—*passionate, impulsive,* and *quick-tempered.*

Perhaps even more important than the above changes is the fact that in 1950, in contrast to 1932, many students were extremely reluctant to take part in the experiment at all. Some felt that to generalize by selecting such simple terms as characteristic of an entire people was a "childish game," if not altogether offensive.

Discussing the findings of these two studies on "stereotypes," Gordon Allport (1954:198) justly concluded that "the 'pictures in our heads' of ethnic and national groups are today less uniform and less cocksure than they were in former years." The reasons for this include the increased interest in the study of social science; the greater tendency for American citizens to travel; the increase in communication among nations and peoples; the more relaxed attitude in the public communication media; and many other varied and complex factors. With respect to the changes concerning stereotypes about the Italians, to the extent that Princeton students represent Americans at all, the difference is also due to the fact that Italians have had more time and greater success in adapting to American society and culture.

Note

1 Building on the work of George Homans (1950), Andrzej Malewski (1965) has produced the following complex proposition to summarize much interesting research in this area of sociology: "If the costs of avoiding interaction are low, and if there are available alternative sources of reward, the more frequent the

interaction, the greater the mutual liking." A less precise version of this proposition is given by Bernard Berelson and Gary Steiner (1964:327): "The more people associate with one another under conditions of equality, the more they come to share values and norms and the more they come to like one another."

Chapter 6 ◉ Assimilation and Achievement

The degree to which Italians have adapted to American society and culture is best exemplified by their achievements with respect to the holy trinity of Modern Graces: Education, Job, Income.

Beginnings and Progressions

We must again take the history of Italians in America into account. The further back into American history one goes, the fewer Italians one finds, but the less humble is their condition in life. The first to come, of course, were the great discoverers, explorers, and experts in the science of navigation. Lawrence Pisani (1957:256) has made the following note concerning early Italians in America:

> First were the great discoverers and leaders of expeditions, and with them the nameless crews of the ships that first sailed to American shores, and the cartographers and navigators who imparted the knowledge needed for the uncharted voyages. Then there were the explorers who set foot on untrod soil and sailed down virgin rivers, the priests who established missions in isolated areas which were later turned into large cities, and the soldiers who, as officers, commanded lonely outposts in the wilderness, and in the rank and file marched with the explorers and discoverers. The Italian fur trader was also there, the paths he followed becoming later the great highways of America.

When new worlds were being explored and conquered several centuries ago, there was no nation of Italy, but only several small states too weak, too poor, and perhaps insufficiently imaginative, to finance large-scale expeditions. The Italians, recognized masters in cartography, mathematics, and the designing and building of ships, had to do their work under the flags of foreign nations. Most accounts of those Italians who blazed the trails to the new continent and then explored it, laying the foundations for the great nation to come, were "hidden under the cloak of history" (Pisani, 1957:14).

In a country traditionally over-concerned with Americanization and Anglicization, little or nothing is known about such figures as Enrico Tonti, who journeyed through the unknown Mississippi region as "strong right arm" and second in command to Robert La Salle; Father Eusebio Chino, who explored much of the Great Southwest; the physician and agriculturalist Philip Mazzei, who, writing in the *Virginia Gazette* under the pen name of "Furioso," had a deep personal influence on Thomas Jefferson and on the political philosophy that fed the American Revolution; Giuseppe Maria Francesco Vigo, wealthy trader, expert adviser on Western defenses, and key personage, both as financier and as military scout, in George Rogers Clark's capture of Fort Vincennes, "the key to the Northwest."

Still less is known of the glassmakers and other artisans who as early as 1610 were invited by the Virginia colony to teach their arts to apprentices recruited from among the settlers. Small, highly skilled groups of Italians initiated the silk-producing industry in several colonies (Pisani, 1957: chapters 1, 2; Schiavo, 1947).

At the beginning of the nineteenth century came the Italian political émigrés, musicians, opera singers, impresarios, artists (among whom were famous sculptors and painters), and with these also vendors of plaster statuary and the (best remembered) organ grinders with their monkeys.

The descendants of these early immigrants cannot be traced today. The culture and, in most cases, the family names brought over from the Old World have been completely fused in the foundry of American culture. The only recognizable Italians in America derive from the multitude of Italian immigrants who have come since the 1880s. As previously noted, these were illiterate functionally literate at best, unskilled, and poor to the point of destitution. When they arrived, most found employment only in the lowliest and least-paying urban jobs.

A relatively small number made their way to the land. Their success has become almost legendary. In New Jersey, they developed berry farms, pepper fields, and vineyards. In western New York they reclaimed the swampy soil and extended their vineyards, orchards, and vegetable farms into the Hudson River Valley. In California, as in New York, they became accomplished wine producers whose wines are now displayed in every wine and liquor store in America. Many thousands are scattered throughout the California fruit belt. In the South, they turned to raising cotton, sugar cane, and rice. In Arkansas, they grew apples and peaches. Sometimes, after nomadic and backbreaking work on the construction of a railroad, Italian workers came upon particularly attractive lands near the right-of-way, which they purchased and made into profitable farms. The Italian colonies in Cumberland, Wisconsin, and Bryan, Texas, originated in this manner. In areas surrounding the metropolitan centers, Italians developed truck gardens to supply fruits and vegetables to the city dwellers in general and to their fellow Italians in particular. Door-to-door vendors and pushcart peddlers established little neighborhood stores, which then grew into larger ones until, in city after city, Italians established themselves among the largest and the wealthiest suppliers of fruits and vegetables (Wittke, 1939:441; Pisani, 1957:72–73).

By far the largest number, however, stayed in the cities. There the Italian immigrant became a common laborer. In New York he replaced the Irish and the Poles on the work gangs building streets, skyscrapers, and subways. His women entered the garment trades; in New York City today more than 50 percent of the labor force in the garment industry is Italian. In Chicago, the immigrant went to work in the stockyards. In New Jersey and New England, he found employment in the silk and textile mills. In Pennsylvania, Illinois, and West Virginia, he worked in the mines. In Michigan and Pennsylvania, he found work in the steel mills. Everywhere in the states of the Northeast, starting at the turn of the century, he contributed the lion's share of toil to the building of roads, dams, canals, tunnels, bridges, and subways. Everywhere he joined and sometimes took control of the street-cleaning force. Many also became gardeners for the better-off.

The immigrants were a hard-working people, out of necessity as well as out of habit and design. At the turn of the century, the most desirable forms of labor typically brought barely two dollars a day. Exploited by *padroni* and poorly paid by employers, they had large families to support and large debts to pay to the usurer. In a great many cases, as previously noted, the immigrants had a driving desire to strike it rich quickly and return to Italy to acquire a sizable plot of land of their own. Then they would have their independence and their self-respect. The utmost energy and industry were required.

The motivation to attainment was most compelling. It is no surprise, therefore, to learn that about 1900, for every $100 earned by native wage earners, the Italian born earned $84, while the average for all other Europeans was only $54 (Handlin, 1951:76). The Italians were lowly, uneducated and unskilled, but they were driven relentlessly toward economic independence! In her study of Greenwich Village, Caroline Ware (1935:394) found that year after year, a smaller proportion of the Italians on the welfare rolls were there because of economic inadequacy than the Americans, the Irish, or other nationalities.

The going was rough, but in keeping with the pattern of all immigrant groups in America, Italian immigrants and their children gradually made room for themselves in the opportunity structures of their society. Accomplishment became easier as the old-timers, influenced by the attractive power of American society and by the rapid Americanization of their children if they were here, decided not to return to the old society. Once they had made this decision, they began to look at the future not in terms of debts to be paid off and little sums of money to be stashed away toward the purchase of a plot of land, but in terms of American criteria of success and achievement for themselves and their offspring.

Nathan Glazer and Daniel Moynihan (1963:206) point out that Italian immigrants "showed a strong inclination for business enterprise" and established thousands of business firms. These include grocery stores; restaurants; dry-cleaning establishments; wholesale food concerns; produce-handling firms; garment factories; and especially trucking and moving concerns, which in a city like New York are almost an exclusive Italian specialty. Their children followed suit or learned a trade in barbering, bricklaying, masonry, cabinet making, plumbing, and various other crafts. In the building trades especially, their early experience as laborers in construction gangs paid off. The old culture had accorded a place of dignity to fine craftsmen. In the village, the mason, the carpenter, the shoemaker had been next to the peasant up on the social ladder, but they had been considerably removed from him. As construction boomed and the services of masons and bricklayers came to be in great demand, many a laborer who had kept his eyes open while carrying mortar and bricks to the craftsmen found it relatively easy to throw away the hod and take up the more profitable and respectable tools of a mason. Children became apprentices to the old-timers and swelled the ranks of the craft. More important still for a few, success in craft sometimes provided a foothold in the contracting business. The Italians' interest in higher education grew as they gained success and security. Most in the second generation graduated from high school, and a few went to college, eventually swelling the ranks of white-collar workers and professional men.

For some of the very enterprising, and perhaps less moral, the bootlegging and related businesses of the Prohibition era provided excellent opportunity for profit. Caroline Ware (1935: 59, 71) found that in the 1920s the liquor business and the speakeasies were the chief new sources of employment and income for the residents of Greenwich Village, especially the Italian residents.

The money made in the liquor business provided a basis for the further development and realization of the Italians' aspirations. There were a handful of cases where spectacular wealth was accumulated this way. A much larger number of Italian Americans made a little money in bootlegging and later invested it in real estate, put up a liquor store, entered the entertainment business, or invested in other kinds of legitimate businesses. Success in these enterprises in turn played an important part in furthering the group's chances for advancement. The entertainment world, for instance, has been a particularly effective vehicle of social mobility for Italian Americans of the second and later generations. The presence of elders of their kind in show business has probably facilitated the recognition of individual Italians' entertaining talents.

Gans (1962:83) makes the interesting point that "most of the successful white singers today are Italians," a fact that, according to him, reflects their "need for display." Whether Italian Americans have a stronger than usual need for display and constitute such a lot of American singers are both points about which one may argue. There can be little argument, however, about the fact that there are many Italian American singers and actors, even though one cannot always recognize them by their surnames. It is easy enough to determine the ethnic background of such entertainers as Sinatra, Como, and Franciosa. It is not so easy in the case of such other Italian Americans as Dean Martin, Connie Frances, and Ann Bancroft.

Sports have also been an effective avenue of achievement for countless Italian Americans. In such sports as baseball, football, boxing, coaching, as well as in several sports-related fields, they have gained fame and money, and hence established a solid basis for further achievement by future generations. Consider such names as Joe Di Maggio, Frank Crosetti, Johnny Wilson (Panici), Rocky Marciano, Willie Pep, Gene Sarazen (Saraceni), Rocky Colavito, and such renowned coaches as Lou Little (Piccolo), Jordan Olivar (Olivieri), and Vince Lombardi.

There is little doubt that what may be termed the *peacock complex* is an important element in the behavior and career of entertainers and athletes in general. But that is hardly an important sociological factor when their success is viewed from an ethnic perspective. Traditionally, participation in sports and show business is among the first and most effective avenues of mobility for members of national and racial minorities. First, these fields offer the promise of large economic gains. At the same time, they are fundamentally *service occupations*. As such, they do not threaten the dominant group's conception of the minority as a socially inferior people. The present-day descendants of the gladiator and the court jester may demand and receive handsome economic rewards for their services, but they neither demand nor receive high social recognition for them. The social value of their efforts will come to full fruition only after they or their children have entered more conventional occupations.

Sociologically speaking, the success of a minority group in sports and show business represents a sort of compromise between the dominant group's tendency to cling to an old conception of group relations and the minority group's drive toward economic and social equality. It follows from this proposition that, *ceteris paribus,* as the minority's "social capital" in the larger society increases, its participation in business, government, and the professions rises and the proportion of its members in sports and show business decreases. This interesting hypothesis deserves the attention of sociologists in general and students of minority groups in particular.

Little by little, the Italians have Americanized themselves. As their accomplishments have multiplied, their success has been met with approbation from the larger society, and the recognition has done more than anything else to improve their conditions. As early as 1939, Carl Wittke (1939:439) could state about the Italians in America:

> To a surprising degree, the Italian has repeated the experience of the Irish. He has risen rapidly from pick-and-shovel work to more skilled trades, and from bootblacking and peddling and barbering to more pretentious business enterprises. The Italian element has now displaced the Jews in New York as the largest single group in the needle industries. Thousands have joined the building trades' unions as masons, carpenters, plumbers, and electricians. Many Italians have become officials in labor unions. Luigi Antonini is head of the American Labor Party of New York. Others are interior decorators, textile designers, and builders of furniture. Italians constitute a

large percentage of the membership in the musicians' union. Some Italian bootblacks have prospered to become "shoe-shine kings," and now control scores of establishments. Fruit, vegetable, and candy peddlers prospered and opened confectioneries, restaurants, hotels, and groceries. A few became importers of olive oil, macaroni, and ravioli, or manufacturers of spaghetti and cheese. San Francisco, Chicago, New York, and other cities have Italian Chambers of Commerce . . . . the second and third generations entered the professions and made a notable record . . . .

An interesting occupational study carried out in New York City in the early 1930s gives a good indication of the occupational mobility of the Italians at a crucial period of their history in this country. John D'Alesandre (1935:11–21) compiled information from the birth, marriage, and death certificates of New York City residents for the years 1916 and 1931 as contained in the original records of the city's department of health. He found a rising tendency toward diversification in their occupations as well as reason to conclude that the recently arrived Italians were already following the occupational pattern set by the population of the city as a whole.

Focusing on data gleaned from birth certificates, for instance, it was found that whereas 50 percent of all Italian workers in 1916 were laborers, only 31 percent were laborers in 1931. More revealing still, when we look at the data from marriage certificates, which concern almost exclusively the second generation, we find that laborers constituted 32.5 percent of the total in 1916 and only 10.6 percent in 1931. In 1931 jobs—like electrician, painter, plumber, contractor, foreman—were claimed that either were insignificant or were not represented at all among Italians in 1916. Small-business jobs and such other job categories as clerk, salesman, baker, plasterer, and painter tended to double or more from 1916 to 1931.

Achievement did not come easily. The inevitable process of amelioration was greatly impeded by several factors. The background of the immigrants is a set of factors that we have already discussed. A second major obstacle, also mentioned already, was the sheer volume of emigration, which made the old-established Americans feel threatened by such a great mass of unschooled and unskilled people. The advancement of Italian Americans was also hindered by historical events. By 1930 many were ready to take a big step into the opportunity structure of their society; but the Great Depression sent many of them to the soup line. With the Depression barely over, World War II began. The war, of course, created jobs and multiplied the chances for obtaining a good income. However, the fact that Italians were on the other side of the firing line in Europe did not help Italian Americans in their competition for the better jobs. In short, hard as it may be to believe, the "era of benevolence and beneficence" for the Italians in America is hardly twenty years old. Only in the 1950s—when the memories of 1940 had faded away, when the third generation had become numerically significant, and when the national postwar economy had established its strength—did the Italians begin to have relatively free access to the promise of America.

Under the Microscope of N-ACH'ers

For social scientists diligently interested in demonstrating that some people prize success more than others, Italian Americans represent a slowly achieving people. To use the imperious language of the trade, Italians have a low "need for achievement" (N-Ach). According to Bernard Rosen (1959:48), there are three components of the "achievement orientation": 1) "achievement motivation," which "provides the internal impetus to excel in situations involving standards of excellence," 2) "certain value orientations which implement achievement-motivated behavior," and 3) "culturally influenced educational-vocational aspiration levels."

Equipped with this conceptual scheme, Rosen turned to his students "enrolled in two sociology classes" and, with instructions never made public, sent them out to sixty-two communities in four states in the Northeast to interview "pairs of mothers and their sons" belonging to different nationality and racial groups. The students came up with 427 such pairs. They included French-Canadians, Italians, Greeks, Jews, Black Americans, and white Protestants. On the basis of data provided by certain batteries of questions, Rosen (1959:60) then concluded that

> the groups place different emphases upon independence and achievement training in the rearing of children. As a consequence, achievement motivation is more character- istic of Greeks, Jews, and white Protestants than of Ital- ians, French-Canadians, and Negroes. The data also indi- cate that Jews, Greeks, and Protestants are more likely to possess achievement values and higher educational and vocational aspirations than Italians and French- Canadians. The values and educational aspirations of the Negroes are higher than expected, being comparable to those of Jews, Greeks, and white Protestants, and higher than those of the Italians and French-Canadians. Voca- tional aspirations of Negroes, however, are the lowest of any group in the sample.

The travails of some social scientists! Look at those unpre- dictable Black Americans. They "intend[ed] for [their] son to go to school" very "far" (the measure of "the values and educa- tional aspirations"). However, when they were asked, "If things worked out so that your son were in the following occupations [ten occupations, from lawyer to bus driver, follow], would you be satisfied or dissatisfied?," a great many of them said they would be satisfied even with the lowest jobs (Rosen, 1959: 59). And this for Rosen indicated a low vocational aspiration —a fact that Black Americans might consider amusing if they did not deem it outrageous. One is reminded of the lamb in the ancient fable who, while drinking from a stream, was accused by the wolf of dirtying his water. That could not be, reasoned the little lamb, because he was downstream from Mr. Wolf. But sweet reason has never been much in vogue. As the wolf saw it, if it was not now, it was last year that the lamb muddied his water. Still intent on keeping the record straight, the lamb pointed out that he was not yet born last year. Well, maybe not, but then his mother must surely have committed the deed. The wolf ate the lamb.

This is not the place to argue against Social-Darwinist falla-cies coated with Weberian fantasies. Nor would it be intellec-tually fecund to demonstrate that, given the great emphasis in our society on what William James appropriately termed the "bitch Goddess, success," any attempt to show that group X has a higher achievement motivation than group Y is to show that group X is more respectable, more American than Y. After all, as Robert Merton (1957:139) pointed out in his brilliant analysis of "social structure and anomie," in "the land of opportunity" "not failure, but low aim, is crime."[1] It is hard, however, to understand why the inconsistency in the position of Black Americans was not sufficient to sensitize the Rosen research team to the grave dangers inherent in interpreting highly charged aspects of human behavior. One cannot imagine the Black American mother of the mid 1950s, end-lessly accused of not raising her children to honor the American Dream, not telling interviewer "Joe college" that she "intended" to send her son to school as long as everyone else did. Nor can one imagine that same mother, possibly married to a man with a long history of unemployment, not being satis-fied with the idea of her son's becoming a department store salesman (*ninth* in status rank on the list of the ten occu-pations!).

Consider, next, the measure of "independence training," one of the "kinds of socialization practices" generating achieve-ment motivation. It consists of the answers to this question, "At what age do you expect your son to do the following things?" Among the things then read off are the following: "To be active and energetic in climbing, jumping, and sports"; "to make his own friends among children of his own age"; "to be able to entertain himself"; "to do well in competition with other children" (Rosen, 1959:51).[2] Rosen found not only that the mean year for "independence training" among Italian mothers was the highest of all six groups but also that, in each group, lower class mothers gave their children their inde-pendence at a considerably later age in life than did upper class mothers.

Anyone familiar with people living in the American slums will be puzzled by these findings and necessarily wonder about

Rosen's conceptualization of "independence training" and the credibility of his information. It is hard to reconcile his findings with certain other data as well as with plain common sense. Herbert Gans (1962:56), for instance, found among the Italian Americans of Boston's West End that once children have "passed the stage of babyhood," parents will talk to them "in an adult tone," "will cease to play with them," will give them "considerable freedom to act as they wish" in their own peer group, and will not "supervise" or "guide" them. Indeed, the "children's world is their own," and "parent-child relationships are segregated almost as much as male-female ones."

Interview data comprise one type of "evidence" to show that French-Canadians, Black Americans, and Italian Americans have a weaker achievement motivation than white Protestants, Jews, and Greeks. Rosen also presents "evidence" consisting of alleged facts about the situation back in the old society. So, for instance, the southern Italians in Italy are pictured as failing to stress "the notion of competition with standards of excellence." Moreover, "in the father-dominant Italian and French-Canadian families, pronounced concern with the child's ability might be perceived as a threat to the father" (Rosen, 1959:52). One might well psychoanalyze the man in the moon! If what one reads about "father dominance" among the British and their German neighbors has any validity at all, one can only have pity for the poor English and Germans, for, despite all their Puritan or Pietistic ethic, they have most assuredly been doomed to abysmal failure.

Elsewhere, we read that whereas "Jews have placed a very high value on educational and intellectual attainment," among the southern Italians, "school was an upper class institution, not an avenue for social advancement for their children, book-learning was remote from everyday experience, and intellectualism often regarded with distrust" (Rosen, 1959:57–58). A similar point was made by Fred Strodtbeck in a related paper in which the Jews and the Italians of New Haven were compared on "achievement." While "Jews have traditionally placed a very high value upon *education and intellectual attainment*," "To the typical Southern Italian peasant, school was an upper-class institution and potentially a threat to his desire to retain his family about him . . . . Family life, local political power, and other objectives were stressed as alternative goals to learning" (Strodtbeck, 1958:150).

It is hard to imagine that "local political power" was obtainable in southern Italy without school learning. To be sure, there must have been cases, as there are certainly today, of uneducated individuals who held the local power in the southern Italian communities of sixty or eighty years ago. However, the fact is that then as now almost invariably the political power was held by the local land baron, the pharmacist, the physician, the lawyer, and other educated members of the gentry.

Moreover, the very convergence of wealth, power, and education in the same person—the local *signore*—could not but lead the peasant to view education as extremely desirable. After all, it was an obvious ingredient of that famous "superiority" that had the power of control over most aspects of the life of those who did not possess it.

Among those who have created countless myths about the society and culture of southern Italy are a number of the more fortunate Italian Americans themselves. Many belong to that category of ethnic people characterized by Irvin Child as "rebels." Generally speaking, they are well-meaning individuals who are particularly impatient about the apparently slow pace of many others in making the cultural transition. Through a "historical" subterfuge these Italian Americans blame the old-timers for their part, however indirect, in hindering the progress of those in the group who have striven with earnestness and anxiety. The swift in a mountain-climbing party are often impatient with their slow-moving associates.

Leonard Covello, one of the great educators of New York City, has said about education in southern Italy and America that

> To the *contadino* parent, education was the handing down of all the cultural, social, and moral value of his society through the medium of folklore, or the teaching, generation after generation, of the child by the parents. The peasant's desire for security in his way of living was directly opposed to education from outside the family

circle. . . . This antagonism toward the school, which was definitely manifested in Italy and which constituted a part of the cultural tradition, was carried over to America and paved the way for the *still current* lack of rapprochement between the American school and the Italian parents [Covello, 1967:403; emphasis provided].

Covello was the creator of "the community school" concept (Wilcox, 1967), which argues that in order to achieve its goal, the school must have a thorough understanding of the culture of the individuals and groups that it serves. Covello was thus naturally led to exaggerate the conflict between the American school and the southern Italian immigrants in order to strengthen his argument for the community-centered school. However, the preceding quote does little justice either to Italian Americans or to the reality of cultural conditions in the southern Italy of sixty or seventy years ago.[3] Moreover, although it was taken from a recently published work, the statement was written in 1944 and was provoked by research done in East Harlem, New York City in 1934, at a time when one of the poorest colonies of Italian Americans was in the grip of the worst economic crisis in American history. Poor people in the mid-1930s were understandably more concerned with procuring the daily bread, even if it meant encouraging their young adults to seek a job, than with the education provided by a slum high school. People do not make a fetish of education when their bellies are empty.

This much can be said about the peasants of southern Italy prior to the great emigration. In general, they were so deprived and so far removed from what C. Wright Mills (1951: 265) termed "the educational elevator" that to entertain the thought of intellectual pursuits amounted, for most, to asking for a miracle. The people of that region, however, have never been against miracles. Any talk of "antagonism toward the school," as Covello argues, or of "intellectualism" being regarded "with distrust," as Rosen claims, is pure poppycock. The peasants distrusted—and they still distrust—*intellectuals* for their constant abuses, *not* intellectualism or learning per se. Remarkable testimony to this fact is the high regard in which the peasant held his peer who was good at storytelling and song-making, or learned in the ways of the world beyond the confines of the little village. Witness, too, the extreme value placed on the priesthood, whatever the hostility toward the institution, as an avenue to economic comfort, social importance, and "intelligence," as peasants even today call formal education.

Nor was the making of a priest (and, on less frequent occasions, a lawyer or a physician) a threat to family unity, as Strodtbeck would have us believe. Why should it have been? In the preponderant majority of the cases, the educated son would spend all his life in the paternal domicile or at best a few yards away. He would be no less drawn to the larger family because of that. In the meantime, the family enjoyed the honor and wealth that derived from the son's education.

The peasant's relation to education in the New World was more complex than most scholars have imagined. Lost and bewildered in the urban jungles of Little Italy, poor and heavily in debt, ever threatened by economic depressions, surrounded by hostile neighbors and gangs, many Italian immigrants were forced to add to their normal distrust of scholarship their disesteem of an irrelevant school. Moreover, as Ware (1935:337) noted, the schoolteacher and what she represented often set the children of immigrants vigorously against the school. The school and teacher completely disregarded the training the children had received in the home, or altogether held it in contempt. They often treated the children as if they were deliberately misbehaving when actually they were conducting themselves as they had been taught in the family. The children of Italian immigrants, fathered by the illiterate, must have had a particularly trying time under the philosophy of "good morning, Mr. Robin." One necessarily wonders how many children pressured the old-timers to pull them out of school and away from endless epithets, humiliations, and brawls so that they might go to work with their father or an older brother and get on with the job of living life among one's own people. Many children found themselves between the proverbial hell and high waters. On the one hand, as previously noted, the school tended to set them against their parents. On the other hand, it sought to mold them anew without the needed reward of social acceptance. Many scholars have documented the reasons that divert the unwelcome children of the poor from school (Hollingshead, 1949; Warner *et al.*, 1944; Fuchs, 1968).

There is still another aspect to this necessarily complex question. In the peak years of the Italian immigration, truancy was not always noted by officials, a practice that made it that much easier for certain classes of children and their parents to get away with it. In New York City, for instance, in the years before World War I public schools were simply unable to take care of the rapidly growing numbers of Italian children throughout the city. Hence, it was extremely difficult, if not altogether self-defeating, to enforce attendance upon the Italian youth (W.F.W.P.W.P.A., 1938:114–115). And many who did not play hooky had to pay, within the classroom, for the problems that their coming had created. Lack of adequate facilities in the public schools led considerable numbers of Italian parents to enroll their children in the parochial schools operated by the Catholic church. Desire for religious instruction played no role in this, for religious training in the old country had been exclusively a family affair. Moreover, in Italy, parochial schools were virtually unknown.

There are still other reasons why Italian immigrants, for a while at least, seemed less than enthusiastic about schooling. In the old country, when one went beyond the five grades of grammar school it was everybody's understanding that the additional education was needed to become a priest, a teacher, a lawyer, or perhaps a physician. In the Italian school system specific training began immediately, and the child was quickly socialized into the culture of his intended profession. But this American high school—what was it? To the average Italian immigrant it must have seemed little more than a playground, a place for endless bickering and fighting, an institution where arrogant teachers produced ill-trained craftsmen or underpaid clerks with little actual education and no more prestige than that which accrued to a carpenter. Leonard Covello (1958) related in his autobiography how his immigrant father told him to go to work upon learning that he was playing sports in school. The old-timer was understood to indicate that he did not give a dried fig for education. This inference, however, is preposterous in the extreme. The gentleman's lack of respect for the American high school was merely reinforced by the incident concerning sports. To this day, in Italian schools no sports are practiced except for an occasional hour of physical education. As Oscar Handlin (1951:253) has colorfully noted, "The worried parents could see no sense in the athletics, the infantile antics of grown men playing at ball."

College, of course, was viewed differently. But college was expensive. Furthermore, the road to higher education entailed the sort of intellectual guidance and home atmosphere that the ignorant former peasants could not provide. Among other things, preparation for college required some counseling on the part of somebody outside the home who knew "the score." Someone had to "discover" the promising child, as the priest or the landlord had sometimes done in the old village. Who could play such a role in the urban jungle? School counselors even today insist on encouraging underprivileged children to take up a trade. W. Lloyd Warner and his associates (1944: 78–80) point out that in Yankee City, a typical New England town, *teachers* very often dissuade lower status students from preparing for college. Usually, they merely "have a talk" with the less fortunate students in order to urge them to be "realistic." But they do not shy away from more forceful techniques, such as failing those who in their opinion should not pursue college-preparatory curricula.

The assumptions teachers sometimes make about their pupils are truly puzzling. Take the cases of a dozen youngsters, personally known to this writer, who came to this country to join their father after having pursued studies in Italy that included between five and eight years of Latin and three to five years of Greek. Upon entering high school, their teachers immediately assumed that they would make good carpenters and electricians, but hardly anything else. Education has a strange way of feeding on itself. For a long time in this country, the school counselor was invariably a Mr. Jones, and sometimes a Mr. O'Connor or a Mr. Goldberg. Mr. Lombardi was rarely to be seen. And the young Lombardis in school had no one to encourage them to reach for the moon.

W. Lloyd Warner and Leo Srole (1945:99) note that an important factor affecting the mobility rate of immigrant groups is "the type of motivation which induced migration to the United States." The Jews and Levantine Greeks, to whom Italians are often compared, are derived from primarily urban classes of merchants and craftsmen, and came with the aim of establishing themselves permanently. By contrast, the Italians were predominantly peasants and laborers who came intending to return home. Walter Firey (1947:188) found that even after twenty or thirty years in this country, only 49.1 percent of the Italian immigrants in the North End of Boston had taken out their citizenship papers. Warner and Srole (1945:99) make the following observation: "Generally, their aspiration was not to rise in status in this country but to secure sufficient funds with which to increase their landholdings and therefore their economic status in the homeland." Not all followed their original plan to return, but for a while "there was little impetus to meet any but the minimum terms of the society." Therefore, although many immigrants "were as quick as any in accepting better jobs, they were somewhat late in selecting better places of residence, and they were especially slow in adapting to the opportunities and demands of class ascent."

Italians came to these shores with plenty of "achievement motivation." Since, however, they did not come with the intention of staying—since they were "sojourners" (Paul Siu, 1952: 34–35), so to speak—ambition was naturally directed in terms of achievements in the home society. Thus achievement motivation of Italian immigrants must be understood in their own particular terms. The extent to which southern Italian immigrants valued their own concept of success may be determined by considering the very large number of those who in the last fifty years have returned home, bought land from the local gentry, and thus have given rise to a good-sized class of independent farmers. Today in southern Italy there is scarcely a village where a large percentage (often a majority) of the landowners are not returnees from the United States.

Even more revealing is that one of the first acts of thousands upon thousands of Italian immigrants was to seek the best opportunities available by sending their children to institutions of higher education *in Italy*. My studies in southern Italian villages have shown that one of the most striking effects of emigration has been the creation of a vast army of teachers, lawyers, physicians, and other professionals who, their training paid for by the proceeds of their immigrant fathers' toil in America, have contributed a big share to the swelling middle class in Italian society (Lopreato, 1967).

"Achievement motivation" represents an extremely complicated theoretical problem. A paper by Suzanne Keller and Marisa Zavalloni (1964:58–70), however, is extremely helpful in illuminating the relevant issues. Keller and Zavalloni have pointed to contradictory findings concerning the relationship between ambition and achievement. They have shown that nothing credible has been established about the relative ambition of different classes, different ethnic groups, and the like. The major difficulty appears to lie in the widespread assumption that the motivation needed to realize certain goals is a constant. The assumption is erroneous because socially desirable success-goals are not equally accessible to all classes and groups of people.

Keller and Zavalloni introduce the concept of "relative distance" in order to clarify the relevant dimensions of ambition and opportunity for achievement and to distinguish "the structural from the personal sources of ambition, and the absolute from the relative values of a success-goal." Thus they (Keller and Zavalloni, 1964:60) state:

Social class alters the content of what is aspired to and thus constitutes an intervening variable between individual ambition and social achievement. Any given success-goal has both an absolute and a relative value, the first referring to the general consensus regarding its over-all . . . desirability, the second, to its class accessibility. In order, therefore, to compare the extent of ambitiousness . . . one needs to know not only the absolute rank-order of a given goal and group rates of endorsement of this goal . . . but also the relative distance of each [group] from it.

Hence, in aspiring to the job of department store salesman, a lower class person may show more ambition than the son of a professor who aims for a professorship. In the latter case the ambition is for status persistence, in the former it is for status achievement.

Likewise, there is a "personality" component of ambition in the sense that even at the same class level some individuals are better qualified and more motivated to achieve certain goals than others. But there is also a "structural" component of ambition. The structural component of ambition to attend college is lower for a middle class individual than for an impoverished member of an ethnic group living in an urban slum. The middle class individual has more and better facilities for pursuing this goal—he need not try as hard as the lower class slum dweller for the same goal.

It is, in conclusion, thoroughly in keeping with the facts to argue that Italian immigrants were not always energetic in guiding their children through the formal educational channels. To reiterate some of the reasons for their behavior: School and teachers were generally hostile to the family. The immigrants saw little or no value in the education provided by the American high school. In school, children were often advised to train for working class occupations, like the trades, which in many cases could be learned more quickly and more effectively on the job at the same time one was making a living. Given the contempt in which the school, a middle class institution, held immigrant culture, the school was particularly effective in inducing a "rebel" reaction among the immigrants' children—the more successful the child was in school, the more likely he was to rebel against parental authority and culture; school attendance beyond a certain level, therefore, entailed costs to family integrity that far outweighed the foreseeable rewards accruing from it. Finally, Italian immigrants often had very low incomes but large families to support; hence, the family group had to look for additional sources of income. Taking in boarders and allowing the wives to work outside the home were two ways of obtaining funds. When for one reason or another the mother could not work, jobs were found for the children. About 20 percent of the families sent their children to work (Pisani, 1957:91).

In fairness to the old-timers, however, altogether too much

has been made of their alleged aversion to education. They had at least moderate respect for it. This can be inferred both from the conditions surrounding their relationship to the gentry in the Old World and from their children's actual achievements in education, occupation, and income.

Where They Stand

Fortunately, there are data available that go beyond mere speculations, and aid in determining the extent to which the Italians have taken advantage of opportunities in the United States.

According to the 1960 U. S. census, the median years of school completed among those born in Italy was only 5.9 years, compared to 8.5 years for all foreign born. Only immigrants from Lithuania and Mexico, of the sixteen nativity groups listed, had completed fewer years. The median number of years for second-generation Italian Americans fourteen years of age or older was 10.9, compared to 11.0 for all second-generation Americans, and 10.7 for all Americans of the same age group (U.S.C.P., 1960:9, 38–41).

It is clear that the Italians in America have not achieved spectacular educational success. But the above findings clearly show that they *have* accomplished what is average in American society. If this fact has not been evident so far, it is because scholars of this nationality group have ill advisedly generalized from what they have learned from highly specialized samples. There has been an unfortunate tendency among students of Italian Americans to do their research in those areas where they are sure to find the subjects of their studies with the least sampling effort. That often means a slum. Gans' study, previously discussed, exemplifies this statistical bias perfectly. Under the circumstances, what observers have found may be relevant to Italian Americans to the extent that they contribute to the national composition of the lower and working classes, but says little or nothing at all about Americans of Italian origin as a whole.

Occupationally, the Italians also hold their own. Despite

all the impediments they have found in their way, 38 percent of the second-generation males held white collar jobs in 1960, with a slight underrepresentation among the categories of professionals, technicals, and kindred workers. On the other hand, 42 percent of the white natives of native parents held white collar jobs (U.S.C.P., 1960:9, 48).

An extremely interesting study by Leonard Broom and his associates (1967) casts further light on this question. Using the 1:1,000 sample of the 1960 census, these authors calculated indicators of rank for education, income, and occupation and compared various racial and ethnic groups on that basis. Taking native whites as the "norm" or point of reference that would be equal to 100 on all three scales, Broom and associates first compared *foreign-born* Anglo-Canadians, Germans, Russians (many of whom are Jews), Greeks, French-Canadians, Italians, and Irish. Their findings indicated that only the Anglo-Canadians were higher on all three scales than the native-white average. Somewhat below the norm were the Germans, scoring about 92 in both education and occupation, and 87 in income. The Irish, next below the Germans in education, shared with the Italians the lowest position in occupation and income, scoring about 68 in each. Russians, Italians, and Greeks presented rather peculiar distributions. The Russians, for instance, were almost on a par with the Germans in occupation, with a score of about 86, but they were right next to the Italians and the Irish in income at 70. Their score in education was low at 64. The Greeks exhibited profiles almost identical to the Russians, with scores of 84 in occupation, 70 in income, and 64 in education. The Italians, as indicated, shared the bottom with the Irish in occupation and income, with a score of about 68 in each factor. They were lowest in education, with a score of 51.

Broom's most interesting findings, however, deal with the second generation (the natives of foreign or mixed parentage) because, when viewed in relation to the previous findings, they give us a fairly good idea about relative socioeconomic achievement among the various ethnic groups. The data, reproduced in Figure 2, show that the highest achievement has been exhibited by the Russians, Greeks, and Italians (in that

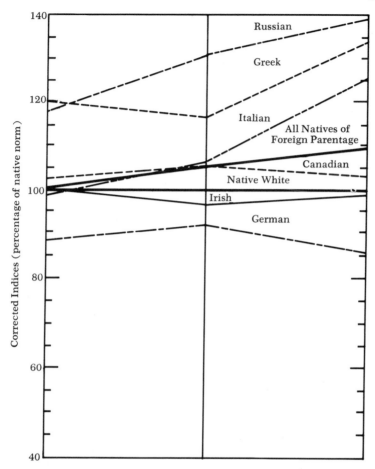

FIGURE 2. *Socioeconomic Profiles for All Natives of Foreign Parentage and for Selected Parentages, United States, 1960.*

SOURCE: Leonard Broom, Cora Ann Martin, and Betty Maynard, "Status Profiles of Racial and Ethnic Populations" (paper read at the meeting of the Pacific Sociological Association, March 1967).

order), while, irony of ironies, the representatives of the "old immigration" rank in achievement either below the native-white norm or only slightly above it. Specifically, with respect to the second-generation Italians, they are at about the norm in education, somewhat higher than the norm in occupation and considerably higher in income.

Broom and associates (1967:8) muse over these findings:

> Perhaps these findings warrant assessment in the light of studies of achievement motivation and vice versa . . . . The implications for public policy are interesting. Among arguments advanced for restricting the "new" immigration from Eastern and Southern Europe was the notion that such persons were inferior to Northern and Western European stock, the "old" immigration. This hypothesis, if it can be so dignified, is not supported by the evidence presented [herein].

We conclude with a sobering thought. These findings do not give the lie to those who have maintained that Italian Americans possess a low achievement motivation *in comparison to some other ethnic groups.* That was really not the issue. What they show is that, despite all the obstacles either carried over from the old country or encountered in America, their achievements in crucial aspects of culture are quite considerable *by national standards.* On the whole they are near or just above the norm represented by native-white Americans. The tendency to compare Italian Americans to especially successful groups to suggest, however unintentionally, that Italians are poor achievers is patently unwarranted by the facts. Indeed, what the facts show is not that the Italians are underachievers but that those ethnic groups to which they are unfavorably compared are *overachievers.* Other groups have in fact succeeded in more effectively partaking of opportunities than the Italians. It is doubtful, however, that their greater success is explicable in terms of greater achievement motivation or a greater appreciation of formal education, increasingly the chief avenue of achievement in modern society. At any given time, most normal persons—whatever their ethnic background—will set for themselves those goals that are highly valued in their society and appear to be attainable *given* their past experience with success and the means presently at their disposal.

It is faulty to assume, as students of achievement usually do, that cultural achievement results exclusively from mental powers and that some people want to get ahead more than others. Rather, it seems obvious that, in addition to the question of differential access to existing avenues of success, different people have different strategies and time schedules for the attainment of the same goals. In the long run, as the wise men of old said, it is possible that "the race is not to the swift." In any case, the emphasis presently placed on will power, motivation, and "need for achievement" when considering the distribution of opportunities in society, or among societies, reflects a Darwinian metaphysics that would be more admirable if it were properly balanced with a more egalitarian metaphysics. It also reflects a preoccupation with "the rat race" that, if what certain sections of our youth today believe is true, empties man too much of his human content.

Notes

[1] Rosen, of course, could argue that he does not share such a value. And we could remind him of the old Italian proverb, "La Lingua batte dove il dente duole"—the tongue always licks the aching tooth, or, the squeaky wheel gets all the grease.

[2] Taken from M. Winterbottom (1958:455).

[3] Scholars in Italy are almost invariably startled by American portrayals of Italian conditions, for they usually bear the same relation to the facts that pizza and spaghetti with meat balls bear to Italian cuisine.

Chapter 7 ⊚ Conclusion

Two questions are crucial in any effort to understand a situation of cultural contact like that created by immigration. One concerns the *processes of assimiliation*, adjustments made by the new arrivals, as individuals or groups, in the receiving society. The other pertains to *responses to immigration*, reactions of the receiving society itself to the addition of new members.

Processes of Assimilation

There are various ways of classifying minorities and their component subgroups. In a widely read paper, Louis Wirth (1945:354–364) suggested that, in view of the world setting around 1945, four major types of minorities may be distinguished. One, the *pluralistic minority,* is characterized by a desire to maintain its cultural identity and uniqueness, while at the same time seeking to live in peace and harmony alongside other groups. The classical example of this type is provided by Switzerland, where one finds Germans, French, and Italians living in relative unity despite their numerous linguistic, religious, and other differences.

Unlike the pluralistic minority, the *assimilationist minority* strives for its complete absorption into an emergent whole that is a fusion of various cultural, ethnic, and racial stocks and traditions. Basically, the aim of the assimilationist minority is roughly something like a "melting pot," a notion quite dear to many Americans—old and new.

A third type, the *secessionist minority,* wishes neither assimilation nor pluralism, but rather political autonomy and complete separation from the dominant group in other areas as well. Examples of secessionist minorities may be found especially, but not exclusively, in areas where peoples have previously been absorbed by conquest: the Lithuanians, Estonians, and Latvians of the pre-World War I period; the Jews of Palestine until recent times; and the Garveyite Black Americans of the 1920s or, perhaps, the "Black Panthers" of the late 1960s.

The *militant minority*, finally, seeks much more than political autonomy. Driven by a feeling of superiority over the dominant group, the minority's goal is to reverse roles with that group. A good example is provided by the Sudeten Germans of the pre-World War II period who, encouraged by the Nazis in Germany, made claims on the Czechoslovakian majority that had reduced it to the status of a minority.

Another way of classifying minority reactions, closely related to the above, is particularly appropriate to the American case. It concerns the minority's *types of response to dominance, prejudice, and discrimination*. The focus here is more specifically on individual members of the minority group. But to the extent that individual reactions are recurrent in the group, we are still dealing essentially with group responses. In the literature a large number of such responses are usually discussed. Those considered basic by scholars include *acceptance, aggression, avoidance, obsessive sensitivity, self-hatred,* and *efforts at ego enhancement.*

Generally speaking, *acceptance,* or "submission," as Peter Rose (1964:131–135) more appropriately terms it, means that the minority group individual complies with the majority group's definition of him as a member of a subordinate and inferior group. As George Simpson and J. Milton Yinger (1965:172–173) have noted, such compliance may be "wholehearted," which is extremely rare; or, more frequently, it can be "specific" to a particular situation or phase of the individual's relationship to majority group members. Again, submission is often "unconscious," manifesting itself in "feelings of inferiority" and even in acts of "self-hatred."

Aggression involves striking out against the dominant group or, in view of the dangers inherent in attacking the "power house," instead turning on some substitute target—the proverbial scapegoat. Ways of striking back include such activities as boycotts, remonstrative newspaper columns, acts of physical violence, inefficiency on the job, withdrawal of deference, and humor.

Avoidance refers to activity that leads the minority-group member away from contacts in which he experiences prejudice or is reminded of his subordinate status. "Passing" and changing one's name and religion constitute one type of avoidance behavior. Insulation from the problems and struggles of one's group; sealing one's self off in a ghetto or a Little Italy; and attempts to obtain political autonomy represent other types of avoidance activity.

Obsessive sensitivity is very common among all minority groups. In its simple form, it may manifest itself in the extreme indignation often shown at ethnic epithets. Italian immigrants and their children, for instance, were easily offended and provoked by such terms as "wop," "dago," and "guinea." In a more complex form, obsessive sensitivity results in an individual with a "chip on his shoulder," inclined to perceive the dominant group member as inevitably acting out of malice toward the member of the minority group (Vander Zanden, 1966:422).[1]

Finally, *self-hatred* and *efforts at ego enhancement* are also extremely common reactions among members of minority groups. An individual manifests the first by expressing aversion and dislike toward his own group. As gross examples, Irvin Child's "rebel" among the second-generation Italians of New Haven and the Jew who engages in vehement anti-Semitic attacks (Lewin, 1948:186; Engel, 1958:75–82) probably suffer from self-hatred. Clowning and ingratiation are milder expressions of this type of response.

Wherever there are feelings of inferiority, *efforts at ego enhancement* will be found. This reaction takes various forms. Underlying them all are efforts to compensate for inferior status or to demonstrate the invalidity of the inferiority attribution in the individual case. Operating here appears to be a variation of what Peter Rose (1957) and others have termed "the exemption mechanism"—an attempt to prove oneself an exceptional member of his group and thus claim an exemption from the status afflictions of that group. A striking example of this type of behavior is sometimes observable when some individuals of the Italian American second generation make eager reference to huge but imaginary property holdings of their parents or grandparents awaiting their return in the old country. A few may go further into this pathetic world of fantasy by informing their listeners that their (semiskilled) grandfather in Detroit or New York was once a count in the Old World.

It may be noted that all of the above responses are possible within the same minority, and, depending on the circumstances, any given individual may exhibit multiple reactions. The Italians have manifested all of them at one stage or another of their Americanization. Acceptance of inferior status has been common. The "rebel," to whom self-hatred was previously attributed, is a good example. Indeed, he is a "rebel" to his ethnic group and "hates" himself as a member of it precisely because he considers his group inferior to the dominant group. Again, aggression is particularly well represented by Child's "in-grouper," and by the delinquent boy, as Cohen terms him, or the "hoodlum," as Toby (1958:542–550) prefers to call him.

Child's "apathetic" reaction is an illustration of the Italian American's avoidance response. It may be recalled that the apathetic individual avoided the psychological conflict potentially deriving from the duality of his cultural milieu by deemphasizing and deemotionalizing the symbols and facts relating to nationality—by avoiding any consistent nationality label. Another form of avoidance among Italian Americans is a certain tendency toward physical isolation. As noted, Italian immigrants tended to gravitate toward the little Italies not only because they were economically convenient and culturally comforting but also because to an extent they insulated their inhabitants from the damning and superior behavior of other groups. Within this context, the "in-group" reaction is obviously an avoidance mechanism. Still another form of avoidance, already noted, concerns the Americanization of Italian names. It is not possible to estimate the number of Italians who have changed their names. It is certain, however, that a large percentage of the second generation, and even more among the third and later generations, have made this change. Many undoubtedly have altered their names out of sheer convenience—the old names were too difficult to spell or to pronounce. Many others, however, have changed them in order to lower their visibility—to avoid ethnic labeling and therefore to increase their chances of success.

The transformation of old world names has been one of the first concessions made by immigrants to forces of Americanization. Upon reaching these shores, or soon thereafter, millions upon millions of immigrants changed their names— or had them changed by irreverent or quasi-literate immigration officials. Sometimes, the change was slight, like dropping a vowel. Other times, it was radical. Often the immigrants did not even know what would make a name sound American. The important thing was to just change one's own name to something else. Handlin (1951:282) relates that the Lithuanians and Slovenes entering the mining fields sometimes took on the names of older settlers, "of the Irish and Italians there before them."

The kinds of adjustments and reactions to dominance exhibited by a minority group depend on a variety of factors. When the minority is also an immigrant group, these reactive factors can be conveniently divided into two broad classes: one pertaining to the old society, the other concerning the new. Taken together, those in the first category fundamentally answer the question, "How much of the immigrants' self-identity and social consciousness is invested in the old society?" Generally speaking, the greater the investment, the greater is the *cost* incurred in making the cultural transition— and hence the greater the recalcitrance toward assimilation. Again, combining those factors pertaining to the new society, they basically answer the question, "How much is the immigrant's culture denigrated by the receiving society?" The more benign the majority's reception of the immigrant, the lower is the cost of his cultural transition.

On the basis of information already presented, it can be readily stated that in the Italian case the first type of cost was low indeed. The southern Italian peasant's experiences in his society were not conducive to a deep identification with it. By and large, he was in that society but not exactly of it. The second type of cost, however, was very great. American society was contemptuous of his manners and his ways. As a consequence, a very interesting phenomenon arose in the Italian American community. Although the old-timers did not come predisposed to assimilation, their identification with the old society was so poor that they were in fact highly assimilable. The hostile nature of their reception by the Americans, however, for a time had the effect of artificially inflating their identification with the old society, so that the first type of cost involved in the cultural transition was augmented.

There is a certain irony in the fact that many southern Italians had to come to the United States *to feel Italian.* The unappreciative way in which they were received forced them for a while to make a national identification, and thus *Italianized* them. Thus it was that in America they discovered Julius Caesar and the Roman Empire; the Renaissance and its artists and scientists; Christopher Columbus, Amerigo Vespucci, and Giovanni Caboto (John Cabot, the Venetian explorer who joined the employ of Henry VII at the age of thirty-four). Their newly found ethnic pride protected them from the worst effects of the gratuitous insults of the majority group. In the process, they took an avoidance posture. We have discussed the "in-group reaction," a form of avoidance, as a second-generation phenomenon and found it in a small number of cases. In the first generation, the in-group reaction was common to the vast majority.

However, as America relaxed, as the immigrants and their children weathered the shock of the first encounters and learned to partake of existing opportunities, a feeling of *being American* was born, almost furtively, but then grew gradually until it became a powerful sentiment. Even those who eventually returned to the old country often retained a vigorous attachment to the republic across the sea and fondly recalled their stay in America on every possible occasion. In short, underlying all reactions to an afflictive minority status was a pervasive tendency which would not be spent, nor for long impeded. It was the tendency toward *assimilation*, toward integration into American society.

As the new society changed, developed, and modernized, so did the immigrant and his offspring. In the meantime, their perspective on the old society remained static and thus lost touch with reality. And so it happened that what once may have been a vague notion, a fervent hope that the new society would somehow be better than the old, soon became a powerful attitude that mixed veneration of the new with castigation, or at least pity, of the old. Let a new arrival from the Old World even today make a criticism of America, however mild, while discussing with Italian Americans the relative virtues of the two countries, and he will immediately learn that "this is a free country" and he is certainly free to "go back" where he came from.

The success of the Italians in America has been so great, almost so unbelievable in their own eyes, that they are almost invariably incredulous, confused, even a bit hurt and resentful in learning that their relatives in the old country have not stood still. It is even harder for them to accept the fact that in some cases the people in the old country have achieved more than their American kinsmen. Upon learning that the son of an old cousin in Italy had just become a physician, a building contractor in the New York City area recently reacted, "When I was a boy in Italy I slaved away bringing pigs and goats to pasture. Now they don't like to work over there anymore."

The suggestion was made earlier that Italian immigrants, and indeed all immigrants, tended to view America as a promised land, "the land of opportunity." They were often harshly disabused of this idea at first, but in the long run this idealistic attitude has been perpetuated and reinforced by those who chose to cast their lot permanently with the New World. Its strength in part flows from old ideologies flourishing in our political structures. In a very large measure, however, it is also the by-product of personal achievement. Although most immigrants started out on the lowest rungs of the occupational and social ladders, their children, aided by higher educational achievements, soon made great, sometimes spectacular, advances in keeping with the economic expansion of the nation. The past fifty years has seen a great swelling of the clerical, professional, business, and government occupations. The children and grandchildren of immigrants have been heavily represented in these new jobs. (Hutchinson, 1956).

As a matter of fact, whatever their original difficulties, immigrants, too, experienced considerable mobility, especially into the small-business categories and the skilled and semi-skilled occupations. In any case, the earnings of the immigrants often made possible a much higher style of life than what they had enjoyed in the old country. The image of America that has developed, as a result, has in many cases been in the nature of what a personal acquaintance from the Old World has called "a glorious feeling." The following statement by a young Italian immigrant brilliantly illustrates many an immigrant's basic response to America as it developed step by step during the course of his Americanization:

I go about the streets to find the great history, to feel the great emotion for all that is noble in America . . . . Even in big city like New York I do not find much monuments to the great deeds, to the great heroes, and the great artists . . . . I do not find the great art to compare with the art of Italy . . . . But one day I see very, very big building. My mind is struck. With all I have seen in Italy . . . I have never seen anything like that! I say, "There is the thing American. It is a giant!"

When I went to night school, I had a good impression to me . . . . I learn little English, and about the American government, and how the people can make change and progress by legislation without the force of revolution, and I like very much this idea. The teacher told me why not to become an American? . . .

I have good impression to become an American. But I do not become American because I think always of the grandeur of the Italy civilization of the past! . . . [Then he falls in love and] . . . I do not wish at all to go back to Italy. I think to take wife . . . . I think about many things, but I think especially about the future. Everything begin to look different. I have not think much about the future before, I have think about the past. Maybe I have a son, it is the future that is for him. America is to be his country. What is the past? It is gone. The future is to come, and I think that when my son shall live I wish it to be some great time . . . . The grandeur of the Italian cities . . . held Italy in the world's highest place for nearly one thousand years. But the world continue . . . . Now comes the great day for America, the great financial, the great mercantile power, and I think with that the great science, the great art, the great letters. Why to live always in the memory of past grandeur? They were only men. I am a man, and my son will be a man. Why not live to be somebody ourselves, in a nation more great than any nation before, and my son perhaps the greatest of any great man?

And I see that big work to build the future. I see the necessity to learn the English, to become the citizen, to take part in the political life, to work to create the better understanding between the races that they come to love each another, to work for better conditions in industry. for health and safety and prosperity, to work for the progress in science, for the better government, and for the higher morality—and it become more pleasure to work than to take the leisure. Suddenly it looks to me like that is the American, that is what the American is always to do, always to work for the achievement. It come to me, like I am born—I am American! [Quoted in Park and Miller, 1921:275–277].[2]

One of the most important, though little discussed, reactions among American immigrants in general, and the Italians perhaps in particular, has been a type of behavior that greatly contributes to the perpetuation of the American Dream, namely, what Melvin Tumin (1957:32–37) has termed "a cult of gratitude" to America. Central to the cult are a distaste for "creative criticism," a tendency to "lose sight of the history of effort and struggle which have been required for past mobility," and, we might add, a tendency toward political conservatism.

There is some evidence to indicate that Italian Americans are being increasingly attracted to the Republican party (Tortora, 1953:330–332) and to the conservative wing of the Democratic Party. Nathan Glazer and Daniel Moynihan (1963:214–215) argue that this conservatism is due, in part, to the Italians' insecurity. They suggest, "The Italian American is still uncertain about his acceptance, concerned about his image, and consequently many—in a style similar to that of other second generations—become more American than the Americans, more nationalist than the Mayflower descendants." Although this reasoning is probably true, to a large extent the conservatism of the Italians in America also flows from a powerful cult of gratitude. A study of Italians in New Haven found that they were significantly more likely than the general population to believe that "in the United States everybody can get ahead" (Lopreato, 1957). Their politics follows a pattern typical of upwardly mobile Americans in general, among whom second-generation Americans represent a sizable proportion. Students of social mobility in the United States and in various European countries have found that upward mobility results in political conservatism in the majority of the achievers. It is interesting to note, however, that while in European countries the upwardly mobile are less often conservative than their new class peers (the old-timers in their class), American achievers actually surpass their present class peers in the frequency of their political conservatism (Lipset and Bendix, 1959:67, 70). Elsewhere (Lopreato, 1967:586–592) this peculiar finding has been explained as a form of gratitude to a society that excessively emphasizes the cult of success and at the same time holds the individual responsible in case of failure. The gratitude, then, flows from a sense of relief that the individual has been spared the sin of failure. It would seem, therefore, that, to the extent that among upwardly mobile Americans may be found many immigrants and second-generation Americans, the ultra-conservatism of our achievers is partly due also both to status insecurity and to a sense of gratitude to America for having made possible the realization of hopes and aspirations brought over from the Old World.

Responses to Immigration

Any effort to discuss the ways in which American society has reacted to the immigration of many and vastly different peoples and cultures will necessarily be linked to several philosophies and views that have prevailed at various times about the proper way to achieve Americanization. This approach is necessitated by the fact that what has actually happened—the manner and degree in which immigrants and their descendants have been Americanized—bears considerable relevance to what has been expected of them in the course of American history. Ethics, history, and sociology can all contribute to our understanding of this problem.

THE "MELTING POT". One of the oldest views concerning Americanization is expressed by the highly suggestive phrase of "melting pot." It appears to have arisen as a response of the English settlers to the early immigration of non-English-speaking, but thoroughly acceptable, people of the northwestern European countries. There is some question about the precise implications of the melting-pot concept. A wide consensus, however, suggests that according to this notion the various Protestant groups from Europe would combine and fuse together, producing a new blend, a new people and civilization, a sort of cultural and biological mix richer and greater yet than any other known in human history.

This enchanting idea was soon adopted by the "new immigrants." Under terrific pressure to prove their worth, often they were only too willing to give up their identity in order to be accepted by the dominant and influential members of the "old American stock." In 1908, Israel Zangwill's famous though mediocre play, *The Melting Pot,* was produced on Broadway, attained immediate success, and ran for months. A frequently cited passage from the play reveals in giddy language the central ideas of the melting-pot philosophy:

. . . America is God's crucible, the great Melting-Pot where all the races of Europe are melting and re-forming!

Here you stand, good folk, think I, when I see them at
Ellis Island, here you stand in your fifty groups, with
your fifty languages and histories, and your fifty blood
hatreds and rivalries. But you won't be long like that,
brothers, for these are the fires of God you've come to—
these are the fires of God. A fig for your feuds and ven-
dettas! Germans and Frenchmen, Irishmen and English-
men, Jews and Russians—into the Crucible with you all!
God is making the American [Zangwill, 1909:33].

And again:

Yes, East and West, and North and South, the palm and
the pine, the pole and the equator, the crescent and the
cross—how the great Alchemist melts and fuses them
with his purging flame! Here shall they all unite to build
the Republic of Man and the Kingdom of God. Ah, . . .
what is the glory of Rome and Jerusalem where all nations and races come to worship and look back, compared
with the glory of America, where all races and nations
come to labour and look forward! [Zangwill, 1909:184–
185.]

ANGLO-CONFORMITY, OR AMERICANIZATION. By the end of
World War I, the melting-pot idea was no longer dear to those
who had invented it, and another old conception, always
present in the background, had come to the fore. The tide
of immigration had shifted from northwestern to southeastern
Europe, bringing throngs of people who were in language,
religion, appearance, and background alien to the early immigrants. Borrowing from the writings of the Europeans Gob-
ineau, Drumont, and Chamberlain the idea that social characteristics depended on racial traits, the "Americanists" produced a succession of books "demonstrating" that the rising
problems of America were due to biological flaws in the con-
stitution of the newer immigrants. The fear of being overwhelmed, weakened, and contaminated by them spurred an
incredible Americanization drive. The idea seemed to be that,
since the unfortunate riffraff from southeastern Europe were
already here, one might as well try to instill the good old

virtues in them as quickly as possible—and hence avoid to a degree the inevitable deterioration of the "old stock."

Indeed, the very fact that the new arrivals often made little effort to cast themselves in the boiling cauldron of the American "alchemist," added to the fears, the prejudices, and the efforts at purification by the old American stock. In the attempt to produce 100 percent Americans overnight, all sorts of federal agencies joined the effort to persuade the immigrants to learn English, take out naturalization papers, buy war bonds, forget their former origins, show their patriotism to America (Gordon, 1964:99–100). "They [the 100 percent Americanizers] bade them abandon entirely their Old World loyalties, customs, and memories. They used high-pressure, steam-roller tactics. They cajoled and they commanded" (Higham, 1955:247).

CULTURAL PLURALISM. The rash of extreme Americanism was destined to be of short duration. In some measure it was extinguished by the restrictionist immigration policies that it produced. The resultant diminishing of the flood of immigrants mitigated the epidemic quality of the social problems accompanying immigration. In large part, too, the Americanization movement, in its most virulent form, was soon made ridiculous by the very economic and political attainments of the minority groups whose quality and desirability the movement had questioned.

The melting-pot philosophy, on the other hand, has been more durable. Indeed, it seems to have produced an interesting reaction widely known under the label of "cultural pluralism." There have always been people who have unfavorably viewed both Americanization and the amalgamation envisioned by the melting-pot idea. Back in 1916, Norman Hapgood (1916:202), prominent author and editor, argued that cultural heterogeneity was beneficial for American society. He pointed out that

Democracy will be more productive if it has a tendency to encourage differences. Our dream of the United States ought not to be a dream of monotony. We ought not to think of it as a place where all people are alike. If in a little town in Italy more geniuses could once be produced than are produced in all the world today, our hope should be to have in a country that occupies almost the whole continent twenty different kinds of civilization, all harmonious.

The individual credited with originating the notion of cultural pluralism, however, is the philosopher Horace Kallen (1915). The central idea of pluralism is that a certain amount of cultural heterogeneity and ethnic diversity is not only pleasing to immigrants or ethnic groups who may be unable to avoid them but it is also beneficial to the society as a whole. The important thing is that uniformity be achieved in such crucial areas of culture as language, love of homeland, and loyalty to the political institutions.

The benefits accruing from pluralism are many. For instance, with respect to immigrants, the retention of elements from the old culture provides a certain insulation from possible cultural shock, and thus constitutes a stabilizing force in the individual's gradual assimilation into American society and culture. As far as the entire society is concerned, pluralism— with its accompanying multiplicity of competing associations, groups, and institutions—serves to undermine the chance of class consciousness and conflict, to distribute and decentralize power, and hence to discharge a condition vital to the maintenance of the democratic order (Kallen, 1915; Etzioni, 1959).

As far as the second and later generations are concerned, implicit in the concept of pluralism is the recognition of the persistence of cultural traits and the possibility of accentuating cultural differences in trying to suppress them. Sociologists, who have devoted systematic attention to the pluralism concept only since the end of World War II, have found impressive evidence of the persistence of ethnic heterogeneity in American society. As already indicated, the works of Ruby Jo Reeves Kennedy and August Hollingshead concerning New Haven, Connecticut, have shown that ethnic and religious endogamy is quite marked decades after the great immigration ended.

On the basis of their study of ethnic groups in New York City, Glazer and Moynihan (1963:17) found reason to argue that forty years after the end of mass immigration,

> someone who is Irish or Jewish or Italian generally has other traits than the mere existence of the name that associates him with other people attached to the group. A man is connected to his group by ties of family and friendship. But he is also connected by ties of *interest*. The ethnic groups in New York are also *interest groups*.

In 1949, after indicating processes by which the original culture of certain rural Norwegians in Wisconsin was defended against assimilation, Peter Munch (1949) pointed out that "cultural assimilation" is not necessarily accompanied by "social assimilation." Similarly Robin Williams (1964:364–365) has argued that ethnic groups may live together in close contact for long periods without any really important assimilation. His study of various American communities has suggested that "separateness in primary social relationships has resulted in a society marked by structural pluralism."

Another sociologist (Gordon, 1964:24–25) has cogently defended the thesis that

> the sense of ethnicity has proved to be hardy. As though with a wily cunning of its own, as though there were some essential element in man's nature that demanded it—something that compelled him to merge his lonely individual identity in some ancestral group of fellows smaller by far than the whole human race, smaller often than the nation—the sense of ethnic belonging has survived. It has survived in various forms and with various names, but it has not perished, and twentieth-century urban man is closer to his stone-age ancestors than he knows.

As noted, Gordon's investigations have led him to conclude that people tend to confine their participation in primary groups and primary relationships to their own *social class within* their own *ethnic group,* namely, to their "ethclass."

What, then, about assimilation in America? By now, it must be obvious that in order to adequately understand what has happened in our society, we must take account of various types and stages of assimilation. Gordon distinguishes seven of these. *Cultural or behavior assimilation* (or acculturation) implies that the new group changes its cultural patterns to fit those of the host society. *Structural assimilation* concerns large-scale participation in the cliques, clubs, and institutions of the host society at the primary-group level. *Marital assimilation* (or amalgamation) signifies large-scale intermarriage. *Identificational assimilation* implies the development in the new group of a consciousness of kind or kinship exclusively with the host society. *Attitude receptional assimilation* relates to a level of assimilation at which the ethnic group encounters no prejudice, while *behavior receptional assimilation* implies an absence of discrimination. Finally, *civic assimilation* indicates an absence of value and power conflict; that is, the newcomers do not raise issues concerning the public life (for instance, the issue of birth control) that involve value and power conflict with the larger society (Gordon, 1964:71).

On the basis of this scheme and a certain amount of data, Gordon concludes that cultural assimilation is likely to be the first type of assimilation to occur when a minority group arrives in America. Moreover, this type of assimilation, which does not imply interaction of the group members with others in the larger society on a primary basis, may be unaccompanied by any other type of assimilation *and* continue indefinately as well (Gordon, 1964:77).

In American society, we have a situation of relative cultural homogeneity combined with structural heterogeneity, namely, a "structural pluralism" that may be properly termed a "multiple melting pot." Three pots concern religion and contain Protestants, Catholics, and Jews, respectively with subdivisions along ethnic group lines. Then there are racial pots and, within these, subdivisions along religious lines. Still another pot is labeled "intellectuals," the true cosmopolitans. Finally, there are pots that contain "substantial remnants of the nationality background communities manned by those members who are either of the first generation, or who, while native born, choose to remain within the ethnic enclosure" (Gordon, 1964:130).

Next to the racial divisions, religious cleavages in American society are the most important—and appearing to some to become increasingly so. Gerhard Lenski (1961:329–330), a student of religion and social differentiation, concludes one of his books as follows:

Currently we seem merely to be drifting into a type of social arrangement which Americans of all faiths might well reject if they became fully aware of all it entails.

This problem should be of special concern to religious leaders. Our current drift toward a "compartmentalized society" could easily produce a situation where individuals developed a heightened sense of religious group loyalty combined with a minimal sense of responsibility for those outside their own group. In a more compartmentalized society there is good reason to fear a weakening of the ethical and spiritual elements in religion and a heightening of the ever dangerous political elements. Such a development would be a serious departure from the basic ideals of all of the major faiths in America, sharing as they do in the Biblical tradition. Hence, on both religious and political grounds, Americans might do well to study more critically than they yet have the arguments advanced by advocates of pluralistic society.

Our study of the Italian American case certainly lends support to the idea that American society is characterized by a high degree of cultural unity combined with persisting ethnic, religious, and structural differentiation. In their aspirations, their achievements, and their behavior in relation to the fundamental institutions of their society, Italian Americans appear to be no different than their fellow citizens. But with respect to participation within the primary-group sphere, especially in the case of marriage, they exhibit a high degree of inbreeding. When they do search for contacts out of their own group, moreover, they are more likely to gravitate toward others who share their religious beliefs. A situation in which different nationality groups fail to freely intermarry is a situation of structural separateness, however much they share a common cultural tradition.

There is no perfectly reliable way to predict what may happen in the decades to come. I am inclined to believe that the advocates of pluralism have overreacted to the notion of the melting pot. It is hard to imagine what was expected by those who have recently questioned the applicability of this concept. There is some question as to whether those who called forth the millennium through the melting pot had in mind a complete biological as well as cultural amalgamation of the American peoples. More likely, they aimed at the sort of cultural unity and moral consensus that white Americans at least have already reached. In any case, it would be hardly reasonable to assume that the biological amalgamation of the great variety of people that make up this society could have been achieved in fifty, sixty, or even one hundred years. One wonders, however, whether in the long run this society, which lays great emphasis on such symbols and aspects of national unity as flag, patriotism, and devotion to cultural heroes, will countenance existing divisions.

It is true, as Robin Williams (1964:364–365) notes with reference to different areas of the world, that group separatism can go on indefinitely in a society. It is also quite likely that in a society as large and complex as this, enclaves of uncommitted groups will develop and persist for indefinite periods of time. The students of pluralism, however, may be exaggerating a phenomenon that is still in the process of formation. The fact should be noted, for instance, that although immigration has slowed down greatly since the 1920s, it has by no means come to a halt. One necessarily wonders what would happen in one hundred years to whatever structural assimilation is going on today, should the country become completely closed to all immigration. It is interesting to note that in New York, which in this century has received few German immigrants in comparison to Italian, Jewish, Irish, and other immigrants, Glazer and Moynihan (1963:311) find that "the Germans *as a group* are vanished."

It is possible that the recent emphasis on structural pluralism represents an attempt on the part of enlightened social scientists, anxious about the uncertain implications of the melting-pot idea, to defend the apparently slow pace at which structural assimilation has been taking place in our midst. People certainly do not enjoy being pushed into fusions of any sort, and no social science worthy of the name could remain amoral in view of a breach of such fundamental freedom.

Sociology is a moral discipline. Its fundamental assumption is that society and culture constitute an apparatus devised by man, partly consciously and partly unconsciously, to cope with the physical and human habitats. This means that at the highest levels of theorizing, the discipline cannot avoid passing judgments—scientific if you will, but inevitably moral in their significance—about the *functionality* of social institutions and arrangements. How well do they serve man and his groups? Are some men served better than others? What is the human cost of social institutions? Do some individuals and groups pay a higher price than others? It is all too obvious that for some ethnic groups with rich moral and religious traditions of their own, the complete amalgamation implicit in the melting-pot idea has a destructive quality that may be too costly to bear.

The concept of pluralism may be particularly attractive to us today because of a widely accepted notion: that a society divided along many fronts is likely to be blessed with superficial cleavages and thus be less unstable than one riven by one or few major fractures. The idea is that group hostilities and conflicts are dispersed and are not likely, therefore, to reach the explosive character envisioned by analyses of class conflict, for instance

Whatever the virtues of this conception, it tends to bury the truly scientific question of the *rate,* if any, at which structural unification is *proceeding* in this society. Obviously, to speak of pluralism without considering possible increments or decrements is to speak of a phenomenon in terms of its qualities and not its quantities. And that does not exhaust the way of science. Time and change are dimensions of crucial significance to the science of man. It is to be hoped that they will be brought into the present issue as fruitfully as they have been brought into others.

Leaving aside the racial question, which presents a problem

beyond the reach of this study, it would seem that today's religious differences are the principal obstacle to a greater amalgamation of the American peoples. It is likely, however, that established religion will be less, not more, significant in the life of future Americans. The ecumenical movement of recent years may well be a first serious indication of a rising feeling that Christianity—many people think Judeo-Christianity—is one and indivisible as a moral institution. Very possibly, what we have observed so far is not a tendency toward greater religious separation and compartmentalization, as Lenski seems to have interpreted the phenomenon, but rather a first major step toward structural unity *by way of religion,* traditionally the first moral institution to be served by man. In other words, religious similarities may have facilitated ethnic crossing rather than circumscribing it.

The possible future weakening of the religious tie may well be aided by another recent event of great historical importance. I am referring to the creation of a Jewish state. One may speculate that the tenacity with which Jews have adhered to their old and rich tradition has been due not only to the necessity of maintaining solidarity in the face of current or imminent persecution but also to the absence of a political body, a nation, that could be trusted as a repository and defender of the sacred lore. The Jew, I am suggesting, has had a great sense of responsibility to his fathers to carry on and defend the cause for which they were persecuted. Such responsibility has been general but until recent years entrusted exclusively to the single individual, his family unit, and the local community. With the creation of Israel, it is conceivable that the responsibility will gradually shift to the Jewish state if its political reality can be assured. If this should be the case, exogamy, which at the present is very low for Jews, will no doubt rise sharply.

This writer is in agreement with Robert Park's "natural-history" theory of assimilation. Park (1950:150) suggested the eventual inevitability of a process, in a situation of cultural contact like that provided by immigration, which moves from *contact* through *competition* for scarce goods and on cultural values among the peoples in contact, through *accom-*

modation, or partial resolution of the conflict, and eventually to full *assimilation.*

Amitai Etzioni has criticized Park's theory, disapproving particularly of Park's use of the term "eventually." Etzioni (1959:255) argues:

> When an ethnic group is assimilating, it is suggested that the hypothesis is supported; if an ethnic group is not assimilating, it is suggested that it has not yet reached the stage of assimilation. "Eventually," one can still hold, every ethnic group will be assimilated. As no time interval is mentioned and the sociological conditions under which the process of assimilation will take place are not spelled out, the whole scheme becomes unscientific.

Etzioni's point is fundamentally unassailable. To say "eventually" is like saying "maybe" and "certainly" at the same time; and that betokens an unfortunate scientific immaturity. Nevertheless, Park's theory, however frail, contains a predictive thrust that most existing sociological theories lack. Etzioni expects from Park a scientific rigor that sociology as a discipline has not yet demonstrated. Of course, that may be unrealistic, but it is desirable. But more desirable still is for present-day sociology to accept that the issue is not so much whether "eventually" is tomorrow or a millennium hence, but rather the speed, if any, at which American society is proceeding toward full assimilation. The task requires periodic measurements among existing minority groups of crucial aspects of assimilation, like associational participation and intermarriage. What has been observed about Italian Americans suggests that such studies will reveal rising rates of structural assimilation. Nothing we know says that there is a point beyond which no more such assimilation will occur.

Notes

[1] See Vander Zanden (1966: chaps. 11–15) for a more detailed discussion of minority reactions to dominance and prejudice.

[2] From the life history of a tailor on the East Side of New York.

◉ References

A.R.I.C. (Abstracts of Reports of the Immigration Commission), U.S. Senate, 61st Congress, 3rd Session, Document No. 747, 1911, vol. I.

Allport, Gordon W. *The Nature of Prejudice*. Garden City. N.Y.: Doubleday, 1954.

Anderson, Robert T. "From Mafia to Cosa Nostra," *American Journal of Sociology*, 71 (November 1965), 302–310.

Anfossi, Anna, Magda Talamo, and Francesco Indovina. *Ragusa*. Torino: Taylor Editore, 1959.

Arias, Gino. *La Questione Meridionale*. Bologna: 1919, vol. I.

A.C.P.I.M.I. (*Atti della Commissione Parlamentare d'Inchiesta sulla Miseria in Italia*). Rome: 1953, vol. I, Tomo II.

Bell, Daniel. *The End of Ideology*. New York: Free Press, 1960.

Berelson, Bernard, and Gary A. Steiner. *Human Behavior: An Inventory of Scientific Findings*. New York: Harcourt, Brace & World, 1964.

Bettelheim, Bruno, and Morris Janowitz. *Social Change and Prejudice*. New York: Free Press, 1964.

Bogue, Donald J. *The Population of the United States*. New York: Free Press, 1959.

Bott, Elizabeth. *Family and Social Network*. London: Tavistock, 1957.

Broom, Leonard, Cora Ann Martin, and Betty Maynard. "Status Profiles of Racial and Ethnic Populations" (paper read at the meetings of the Pacific Sociological Association, March 1967).

Campisi, Paul J. "Ethnic Family Patterns: The Italian Family in the United States," *American Journal of Sociology*, 53 (May 1948), 443–449.

Child, Irvin L. *Italian Or American? The Second Generation in Conflict*. New Haven: Yale University Press, 1943.

Cohen, Albert K. *Delinquent Boys*. New York: Free Press, 1955.

Cooley, Charles H. *Social Organization*. New York: Scribner, 1909.

Coser, Lewis A. *The Functions of Social Conflict*. New York: Free Press, 1956.

Covello, Leonard. *The Heart is the Teacher*. New York: McGraw-Hill, 1958.

———. *The Social Background of the Italo-American School Child*. Leiden: E. J. Brill, 1967.

Cressey, Donald R. "Crime," in Robert K. Merton and Robert A. Nisbet, (eds.), *Contemporary Social Problems*. 2nd ed. New York: Harcourt, Brace & World, 1966, 136–192.

Dahrendorf, Ralf. *Class and Class Conflict in Industrial Society*. Stanford, Calif.: Stanford University Press, 1959.

D'Alesandre, John J. "Occupational Trends of Italians in New York City," *Italy-America Monthly*, 2 (February 1935), 11–21.

dal Pane, Luigi. *La Questione del Commercio dei Grani nel Settecento in Italia*. Milano; 1932, vol. I.

Davie, Maurice R. *Refugees in America*. New York: Harper & Row, 1947.

———. *World Immigration*. New York: Macmillan, 1946.

Di Donato, Pietro. *Christ in Concrete*. Indianapolis: Bobbs-Merrill, 1937.

Divine, Robert A. *American Immigration Policy, 1924–1952*. New Haven: Yale University Press, 1957.

Dotson, Floyd. "Patterns of Voluntary Association among Urban Working-Class Families," *American Sociological Review*, 16 (October 1951) 687–693.

Durkheim, Emile. *The Elementary Forms of the Religious Life*. New York: Macmillan, 1915.

Engel, Gerald, Harriet E. O'Shea, Myron A. Fischl, and Geraldine M. Cummings. "An Investigation of Anti-Semitic Feelings in Two Groups of College Students: Jewish and Non-Jewish," *Journal of Social Psychology*, 48 (August 1958), 75–82.

Etzioni, Amitai. "The Ghetto: A Re-evaluation," *Social Forces*, 37 (March 1959), 255–262.

Fenton, Edwin. *Immigrants and Unions, A Case Study: Italians and American Labor, 1870–1920*. (unpublished Ph.D. dissertation, Harvard University, 1957).

Firey, Walter. *Land Use in Central Boston*. Cambridge, Mass.: Harvard University Press, 1947.

Foerster, Robert F. *The Italian Emigration of Our Times*. Cambridge, Mass.: Harvard University Press, 1919.

Fortunato, Giustino. "Povertà Naturale del Mezzogiorno," in Bruno Caizzi, (ed.), *Antologia della Questione Meridionale*. Milano: Edizioni di Comunità, 1955, 159–173.

———. "Il Problema Demaniale," in Rosario Villari, (ed.), *Il Sud nella Storia d'Italia*. Bari: Laterza, 1963, 161–170.

————. "La Questione Demaniale nell'Italia Meridionale, 1879," in Giustino Fortunato (ed.), *Il Mezzogiorno e lo Stato Italiano*. Bari: Editori Laterza, 1911, vol. I.

Franchetti, Leopoldo, "Relazione della Commissione Reale per i Demani Comunali nelle Provincie del Mezzogiorno," in Leopoldo Franchetti (ed.), *Mezzogiorno e Colonie*. Firenze: 1950.

Fuchs, Estelle. "How Teachers Learn to Help Children Fail," *Trans-action*, 5 (September 1968), 45–49.

Gans, Herbert J. *The Urban Villagers: Group and Class in the Life of Italian Americans*. New York: Free Press, 1962.

Genovesi, Antonio. "Il Problema della Terra," in Rosario Villari (ed.), *Il Sud nella Storia d'Italia*. Bari: Editori Laterza, 1963, 3–11.

Gilbert, G. M. "Stereotype Persistence and Change among College Students," *Journal of Abnormal and Social Psychology*, 46 (April 1951), 245–254.

Gini, Corrado. *Nascita, Evoluzione e Morte della Nazioni*. Rome: Littorio, 1930.

Glazer, Nathan, and Daniel P. Moynihan. *Beyond the Melting Pot*. Cambridge, Mass.: Massachusetts Institute of Technology Press, 1963.

Golino, Carlo L. "On the Italian 'Myth' of America," *Italian Quarterly*, 3 (Spring 1959), 19–33.

Gordon, Milton M. *Assimilation in American Life*. New York: Oxford University Press, 1964.

Gottmann, Jean. *Megalopolis: The Urbanized Northeastern Seaboard of the United States*. New York: Twentieth Century Fund, 1961.

Grebler, Leo. *Housing Market Behavior in a Declining Area*. New York: Columbia University Press, 1952.

Green, Arnold W. "The 'Cult of Personality' and Sexual Relations," in Norman W. Bell and Ezra F. Vogel (eds.), *A Modern Introduction to the Family*. New York: Free Press, 1960, 608–615.

Gugino, Carlo Sciortino. *Coscienza Collettiva e Giudizio Individuale nella Cultura Contadina*. Palermo: U. Manfredi Editore, 1960.

Handlin, Oscar. *The Uprooted*. New York: Grosset & Dunlap, 1951.

Hapgood, Norman. "The Jews and American Democracy," *The Menorah Journal*, 2 (October 1916).

Higham, John. *Strangers in the Land*. New Brunswick, N.J.: Rutgers University Press, 1955.

Hobsbawn, E. J. *Social Bandits and Primitive Rebels*. New York: Free Press, 1959.

Hollingshead, August B. "Cultural Factors in the Selection of

Marriage Mates," *American Sociological Review,* 15 (October 1950), 619–627.

———. *Elmtown's Youth.* New York: Wiley, 1949.

———, and Frederick C. Redlich. *Social Class and Mental Illness.* New York: Wiley, 1958.

Homans, George C. *The Human Group.* New York: Harcourt, Brace, & World, 1950.

Hutchinson, E. P. *Immigrants and Their Children: 1850–1950.* New York: Wiley, 1956.

ISTAT (Istituto Centrale di Statistica). *Annuario Statistico Italiano, 1962.* Rome: 1963.

———. *Sommario di Statistiche Storiche Italiane, 1861–1955.* Rome; 1958.

Kallen, Horace M. "Democracy Versus the Melting-Pot," *The Nation,* 100 (February 18 and 25, 1915), 190–194, 217–220.

Katz, Daniel, and Kenneth Braly. "Racial Stereotypes of One Hundred College Students," *Journal of Abnormal and Social Psychology,* 28 (October–December 1933), 280–290.

Keller, Suzanne, and Marisa Zavalloni. "Ambition and Social Class: A Respecification," *Social Forces,* 43 (October 1964), 58–70.

Kennedy, Edward M. "The Immigration Act of 1965," *The Annals of the Academy of Political and Social Science,* 367 (September 1966), 137–149.

Kennedy, Ruby Jo Reeves. "Single or Triple Melting Pot? Intermarriage in New Haven, 1870–1950," *American Journal of Sociology,* 58 (July 1952), 56–59.

Koren, John. "The Padrone System and Padrone Banks," U.S. Department of Labor, Bulletin No. 9, 2 (March 1897), 113–129.

Kraus, Albert L. "Equal But Separate," *New York Times* (July 17, 1968), pp. 55, 61.

Landesco, John. *Organized Crime in Chicago.* Part III of the *Illinois Crime Survey.* Chicago, Ill.: Illinois Association for Criminal Justice, 1929. (Cited in Robert E. L. Faris. *Social Disorganization.* New York: Ronald Press, 1948, 151.)

Leavitt, Marie. *Report on the Sicilian Colony in Chicago,* (unpublished manuscript), in Robert E. Park and Herbert A. Miller, *Old World Traits Transplanted.* New York: Harper & Row, 1921.

Lenski, Gerhard. *The Religious Factor.* Garden City, N.Y.: Doubleday, 1961.

Lewin, Kurt. *Resolving Social Conflicts.* New York: Harper & Row, 1948.

Lipari, Marie. "The Padrone System: An Aspect of American Economic History," *Italy-America Monthly*, 2 (April 1935), 4–10.

Lipset, Seymour M., and Reinhard Bendix. *Social Mobility in Industrial Society*. Berkeley: University of California Press, 1959.

Livi-Bacci, Massimo. *L'immigrazione e l'assimilazione degli italiani negli Stati Uniti secondo le statistiche demografiche americane*. Milano: Editore Giuffrè, 1961.

Lopreato, Joseph. "Differential Assimilation among New Haven Italians," (unpublished paper, 1957).

———. *Peasants No More*. San Francisco: Chandler, 1967.

———. "Upward Social Mobility and Political Orientation," *American Sociological Review*, 32 (August 1967), 586–592.

Lundberg, Ferdinand. *America's 60 Families*. New York: Vanguard, 1937.

Luzzatto-Fegiz, Pierpaolo. *Il Volto Sconosciuto dell'Italia*. Milano: Dott. A. Giuffrè, 1956.

Malewski, Andrzej. "Levels of Generality in Sociological Theory," Referred to in Hans L. Zetterberg. *On Theory and Verification in Sociology*. Totowa, N.J.: Bedminster Press, 1965, 66.

Mangione, Jerre. *Mount Allegro*. Boston: Houghton Mifflin, 1942.

Mann, Arthur. *La Guardia: A Fighter Against His Times, 1882–1933*. Philadelphia: Lippincott, 1959.

———. *La Guardia Comes to Power*. Philadelphia: Lippincott, 1965.

Merton, Robert K. *Social Theory and Social Structure*. New York: Free Press, 1957.

Mills, C. Wright. *The Power Elite*. New York: Oxford University Press, 1956.

Monticelli, Giuseppe Lucrezio. "Italian Emigration: Basic Characteristics and Trends with Special Reference to the Last Twenty Years," *The International Migration Review*, 1 (Summer 1967), 10–24.

Moss, Leonard W., and Stephen C. Cappannari. "Estate and Class in a South Italian Hill Village," *American Anthropologist*, 64 (April 1962), 287–300.

Munch, Peter A. "Social Adjustment among Wisconsin Norwegians," *American Sociological Review*, 14 (December 1949), 780–787.

Musmanno, Michael A. *The Story of the Italians in America*. Garden City, N.Y.: Doubleday, 1965.

Myers, Jerome K. "Assimilation to the Ecological and Social Systems of a Community," *American Sociological Review*, 15 (June 1950), 367–372.

────, and Bertram H. Roberts. *Family and Class Dynamics in Mental Illness*. New York: Wiley, 1959.

Nelli, Humbert S. "Italians and Crime in Chicago: The Formative Years, 1890–1920," *American Journal of Sociology,* 74 (January 1969), 373–391.

────. "Italians in Urban America: A Study in Ethnic Adjustment," *International Migration Review,* 1 (Summer 1967), 38–55.

Neufeld, Maurice F. *Italy: School for Awakening Countries.* Ithaca, N.Y.: New York State School of Industrial and Labor Relations, Cornell University, 1961.

Panunzio, Constantine M. *The Soul of an Immigrant.* New York: Macmillan, 1921.

Pareto, Vilfredo. *The Mind and Society.* New York: Harcourt, Brace & World, 1935.

Park, Robert E. "Assimilation, Social," in Edwin R. A. Seligman and Alvin Johnson (eds.), *Encyclopedia of the Social Sciences.* New York: Macmillan, 1930.

────. *Race and Culture.* New York: Free Press, 1950.

────, and Ernest W. Burgess. *Introduction to the Science of Sociology.* Chicago: University of Chicago Press, 1921.

────, and Herbert A. Miller. *Old World Traits Transplanted.* New York: Harper & Row, 1921.

Pisani, Lawrence F. *The Italian in America.* New York: Exposition Press, 1957.

Potvin, Raymond H., Charles F. Westoff, and Norman B. Ryder. "Factors Affecting Catholic Wives' Conformity to their Church Magisterium's Position on Birth Control," *Journal of Marriage and the Family,* 30 (May, 1968), 263–272.

Preziosi, Giovanni. *Gl'italiani negli Stati Uniti del Nord.* Milan: 1909.

Rainwater, Lee. *And the Poor Get Children.* Chicago: Quadrangle Books, 1960.

Redfield, Robert, Ralph Linton, and Melville J. Herskovits. "Memorandum for the Study of Acculturation," *American Anthropologist,* 38 (January–March, 1936), 149–152.

R.P.C.I.N. (Report of the President's Commission on Immigration and Naturalization). *Whom Shall We Welcome.* January 1953.

Rose, Peter I. "The Exemption Mechanism: A Conceptual Analysis" (unpublished M. A. thesis, Cornell University, 1957).

────. *They and We.* New York: Random House, 1964.

Rosen, Bernard C. "Race, Ethnicity, and the Achievement Syndrome," *American Sociological Review,* 24 (February 1959), 47–60.

Saraceno, Pasquale. "La Mancata Unificazione Economica Italiana a Cento Anni dall'Unificazione Politica," in Biblioteca della Rivista "Economia e Storia." *L'Economia Italiana dal 1861 al 1961,* Milano: Dott. A. Giuffrè Editore, 1961.

Schiavo, Giovanni E. *Italian-American History.* New York: The Vigo Press, 1947.

Silone, Ignazio. *Fontamara.* London: Methuen, 1934.

Simmel, Georg. *Conflict.* New York: Free Press, 1955.

Simmons, Leo. *Sun Chief.* New Haven: Yale University Press, 1942.

Simpson, George A., and J. Milton Yinger. *Racial and Cultural Minorities.* 3rd ed. New York: Harper & Row, 1965.

Siu, Paul C. P. "The Sojourner," *American Journal of Sociology,* 58 (July 1952), 34–44.

Smith, Sandy. "The Mob," *Life,* 63 (September 1, 8, 1967), 15–22, 42B–45, 91–104.

Stonequist, Everett V. *The Marginal Man.* New York: Scribner, 1937.

Strodtbeck, Fred L. "Family Interaction, Values, and Achievement," in Marshall Sklare (ed.), *The Jews: Social Patterns of an American Group.* New York: Free Press, 1958, 147–165.

Sumner, William G. *Folkways.* Boston: Ginn., 1906.

SVIMEZ. *Un Secolo di Statistiche Italiane: Nord e Sud (1861–1961).* Rome; 1961.

Toby, Jackson. "Hoodlum or Business Man: An American Dilemma," in Marshall Sklare (ed.), *The Jews: Social Patterns of an American Group.* New York: Free Press, 1958, 542–550.

Tortora, Vincent R. "Italian Americans, Their Swing to G.O.P.," *The Nation,* 177 (October 24, 1953), 330–332.

Tumin, Melvin M. "Some Unapplauded Consequences of Social Mobility in a Mass Society," *Social Forces,* 36 (October 1957), 32–37.

U.S. Bureau of the Census. *Statistical Abstract of the United States.* 1941 and 1968.

U.S.C.P. (United States Census of Population, 1960). *Subject Reports: Nativity and Parentage: Social and Economic Characteristics of the Foreign Stock by Country of Origin.* Washington, D.C.: U.S. Department of Commerce, Bureau of Census.

Vander Zanden, James W. *American Minority Relations.* 2nd ed. New York: Ronald Press, 1966.

Velikonja, Joseph. "Italian Immigrants in the United States in the Mid-Sixties," *International Migration Review,* 1 (Summer 1967), 25–38.

Vöchting, Friedrich. *La Questione Meridionale.* Naples: Istituto Meridionale del Mezzogiorno, 1955.

Ware, Caroline F. *Greenwich Village.* New York: Harper & Row, 1935.

Warner, W. Lloyd, Robert J. Havighurst, and Martin B. Loeb. *Who Shall Be Educated?* New York: Harper & Row, 1944.

Warner, W. Lloyd, and Leo Srole. *The Social Systems of American Ethnic Groups.* New Haven: Yale University Press, 1945.

W.F.W.P.W.P.A. (Workers of the Federal Writers' Project, Works Progress Administration). *The Italians of New York.* New York: Random House, 1938.

Whyte, William Foote. "Race Conflicts in the North End of Boston," *New England Quarterly,* 12 (December 1939), 623–642.

————. *Street Corner Society.* Chicago: University of Chicago Press, 1943.

Wilcox, Preston R. "Teacher Attitudes and Student Achievement," *Teachers College Record,* 68 (February 1967), 371–379.

Wiley, Norbert F. "The Ethnic Mobility Trap and Stratification Theory," *Social Problems,* 15 (Fall 1967), 147–159.

Williams, Robin M., Jr. *The Reduction of Inter-Group Tensions.* New York: Social Science Research Council, Bulletin 57, 1947.

————. *Strangers Next Door.* Englewood Cliffs, N.J.: Prentice-Hall, 1964.

Winterbottom, M. "The Relation of the Need for Achievement to Learning Experiences in Independence and Mastery," in John W. Atkinson (ed.), *Motives in Fantasy, Action, and Society.* Princeton, N.J.: Van Nostrand, 1958, 453–478.

Wirth, Louis. "The Problem of Minority Groups," in Ralph Linton, (ed.), *The Science of Man in the World Crisis.* New York: Columbia University Press, 1945, 347–372.

Wittke, Carl. *We Who Built America: The Saga of the Immigrant.* Englewood Cliffs, N.J.: Prentice-Hall, 1939.

Zangwill, Israel. *The Melting Pot.* New York: Macmillan, 1909.

Zorbaugh, Harvey Warren. *The Gold Coast and the Slum.* Chicago: The University of Chicago Press, 1929.

◉ Index

About the Author

Joseph Lopreato is Professor and Chairman of the Department of Sociology at The University of Texas at Austin. He has also taught at the University of Massachusetts, the University of Connecticut, and the University of Rome. Dr. Lopreato is the author of *Vilfredo Pareto* (1965), *Peasants No More* (1967), and a forthcoming book on social classes, and has published articles in various Italian journals and in English in *The American Sociological Review, The American Journal of Sociology,* and others.